Advance Praise for *Dinner for Busy Moms*

"Thanks to *Dinner for Busy Moms*, the words 'dinner' and 'moms' together no longer need to inspire dread, panic, or pizza. Let Jeanne Muchnick's 1,001 ideas show you how the evening meal can be made easy, nutritious, and fun—so instead of it making you feel tired or guilty, you can sit back and enjoy both your food and your kids."

—Paula Spencer, *Woman's Day* "Momfidence" columnist and the author of *Momfidence*

"Reading this book made me hungry, and actually motivated me to go to the food store with a list and a meal plan. I also love the tone: It's fun, witty and honest, and as a busy mom of four, I can relate 100%."

—Marian Edelman Borden, author of *The Everything Baby's First Year Book* and *The Pocket Idiot's Guide to Play Groups*

"I love Jeanne Muchnick's step-by-step approach to feeding your family and their collective well-being. I'm a huge fan of planning, especially meal planning—heck, it helped my family and me save thousands of dollars a year when we became suddenly frugal. If you follow Muchnick's advice, you will not only get dinner on the table without stressing yourself out, but you'll also benefit from having that important family meal time together."

—Leah Ingram, author of *Suddenly Frugal: How to Live Happier and Healthier for Less*

"If the Food Network makes your eyes glaze over, but you still want to cook good food for your family, this book is for you. Filled with sanity-saving tips for busy 21st century moms, *Dinner for Busy Moms* is the handy guide to preparing family meals that you wish you had whenever you're staring down the supermarket checkout aisle at dinnertime."

—Jen Singer, author of the *Stop Second-Guessing Yourself* guides to parenting

"Finally, an author who 'gets' that's it's impossible for multi-tasking mothers to get a family dinner together between ballet lessons and soccer practice—and then tells us precisely how to make that dinner happen regularly. Hooray for Jeanne Muchnick."

—Rona Gindin, host of *On Dining* and author of *The Little Black Book of Walt Disney World: The Essential Guide to All the Magic*

"If, like me, you're a mom who would rather scratch her eyes out than cook dinner for her kids, this book is for you. I especially loved the chapter titled, "Feed Yourself First." This book is all about helping moms find shortcuts and encouraging us to indulge ourselves. Plus, any book that advises a chocolate break is a book I want to read!"

—Melissa Chapman, *Staten Island Advance Kids in the City* columnist, *Time Out NY Kids* contributing writer, and WCBSTV parenting blogger

"If there's anyone I've come to trust regarding mealtime and my family, it's Jeanne Muchnick. As an avid fan of her restaurant reviews in *InTown Magazine, Westchester Magazine* and *The Journal News*, this mom of two is my barometer for great food finds. Kudos to Muchnick for taking her keen sense of delectable dining experiences and bringing it to the dinner table."

—Beth Feldman, author of *See Mom Run* (Plain White Press) and founder of RoleMommy.com

"Moms want things that work. From appliances to weight loss programs, we have no time for trial and error. *Dinner for Moms* proves that family dinners work—to raise better students, healthier eaters, and happier people. Jeanne Muchnick reminds us (without laying on any guilt) that it's about the table, not the stove. Passing the peas just took on vital, daily importance."

—Kim Orlando, founder of TravelingMom.com and the TravelingMom Blogger Network

"What's on the menu tonight? According to the author, it doesn't have to be fast food eaten in the car. In fact, experts tell us that parent-child meals around the kitchen table can benefit your children in a myriad of ways without you having to channel your inner Martha Stewart. Breakfast for dinner? Picnics in the family room? Why not? This book explains in an honest and accessible way how to improve your family meals without causing you more stress. And it does so mom-to-mom, which is always how the best advice gets passed, just like a treasured recipe. So dig in to this meaty meal of advice, fun, and common sense. The result is a smorgasbord of benefits every parent can really sink their teeth into."

—Liza N. Burby, publisher of *Long Island Parent* magazine.

You:
A crazed, multi-tasking mom trying to juggle it all with little time for grocery shopping, let alone prepping and planning

This Book:
Frank and fun advice for making mealtimes manageable

Dinner

for Busy Moms

By Jeanne Muchnick

From one busy mom to another.

ISBN 978-1936005000
Library of Congress Control Number: 2001012345

Design by Katie Schlientz, KatieSchlientz.com
Cover Images: ©ISTOCK.COM/RICHVINTAGE
Author photograph by Mark Liflander

Plain White Press books are available at special discounts when
purchased in bulk for premiums and sales promotions, as well as
for fund-raising and educational use. Special editions or book
excerpts can also be created to specifications. For details contact
Publisher@PlainWhitePress.com.

plain white press™

dedication

In memory of my mom, Adele Goldstein Muchnick, whose cooking always lured me to the dinner table. And to my daughters, Corey and Sydney Rosen, and my nieces, Arin and Lily Pieramici—I hope Grandma Dell's recipes and this book's sage advice keep you talking, eating, sharing and laughing always.

acknowledgements

Where to start? It's been a dream of mine to write a book for so long, that now that the moment is here, I can't help feeling like I'm at the Oscars with a laundry list of people I need to thank. So here goes, keeping in mind that if I could, I'd mention everyone, starting with my Pikesville High School English teacher, who always told me I had potential (thanks Mrs. Fowler).

Of course, I couldn't have done any of this without the support of my husband, Mark, and my daughters Corey, and Sydney, who have patiently (for the most part) put up with my "crazed" deadline-infused moods and my gastronomical shortfalls. Huge hugs and kisses, also, to my friends Elisha, Melanie, Chris Ann, Cornelia, Katie, and MaryLynn, as well as my fabulous sister, Ann, and my nieces Arin and Lily, who helped test recipes, as well as did their fair share of proofreading and honest critiquing.

Appreciation and credit also go to the many mom bloggers and nutrition experts who shared their comments and busy mom solutions. Special shout-outs to Martha Marino, the Director of Nutrition Affairs Communications at the Lynnwood, Washington-based Washington State Dairy Council, who offered valuable statistics and research, and Denver nutritionist Julie Hammerstein, who patiently waded through my countless volley of emails as I asked for about the 100th time: *Are you sure this is right?* Beth Oden, a nutritionist in Boulder, Colorado, also lent her words of wisdom, especially with regard to kids and allergies, while O'Fallon, Illinois-based dietitian Laurie Beebe offered innumerable constructive suggestions. And NYC-based Melinda Beaulieu, a certified natural foods chef, lent her advice on feeding complicated (read picky) families. I couldn't have written half of this book without you amazing women and appreciate the hours you spent explaining the differences between canned vs. frozen, low-fat vs fat-free, natural vs. organic, as well as your thoughts and analysis on why the family dinnertime is so sacred. Thanks, too, to

Julie Freedman Smith of Calgary, Canada-based Parenting Power™ who gave me ideas on how to turn off the TV, and to Ellyn Satter who graciously allowed me to reprint her mealtime tactics.

Because I gained about five pounds testing the recipes in the back of the book and got hungrier by the chapter, I have to thank my fabulous photographer, Mark Liflander (LiflanerPhotography.com) who did his best to make me look fit despite the growing mid-section bulge. Heaps of gratitude, too, to Dody Chang, for doing her best to keep me in a Zen state of mind.

An extra portion of recognition to my publisher (and busy mom of twins) Julie Trelsted and her staff at Plain White Press, in particular Roberta Hendry, who were encouraging, insightful, and tolerant—and hopefully caught all my spelling and punctuation errors. We hatched a lot of ideas and debated many a chapter title over Julie's kitchen table, so thank you, Julie—and thank you to her family—who basically "lent" her to me during the birth of this project. An oversized glass of red wine in "cheers" to art director extraordinaire Katie Schlienz, who promptly responded to my cries for help in the form of all-hours-of-the-night emails and technological snafus. Heck, she even made ME dinner! (This is where I need to do a plug for her and her stationery/graphic arts business, so check her out at KatieSchlientz.com.)

A plug, too, to Pam Koner, founder of Family-to-Family.org, which helps feed needy families. She reminds us that we should never take the food we have on our table for granted. A portion of this book's profits will go towards her charity.

Finally, though they're not on this earth anymore, thanks to my parents, Adele Goldstein Muchnick and Beryl Harry Muchnick, for nurturing and comforting me over the years with conversation and bowls of matzo ball soup, brisket, kugel, crab-cakes, mashed potatoes, and more at our Baltimore home. I miss you more than words can say, and only hope one day my girls will read this book with the same appreciation for the ritual of family mealtimes that you both instilled in me.

This Book Can Help You Feed Others

Family-to-Family was started by Pam Koner, a single mom of two teenage girls who got the idea of connecting families with more to those with less after reading a story in *The New York Times* about Pembroke, Illinois, one of the country's poorest communities. When she learned that the food pantries there ran out of food at the end of each month, she decided she had to do something.

Koner contacted the local pastor mentioned in the article to ask how she could match up families in her hometown of Hastings-on-Hudson, NY with families in Pembroke. Within one month she had linked a total of 34 families. That was seven years ago. Today, the organization has grown to include approximately 400 donor families who send monthly food shipments to families in 17 communities in 15 states. Volunteers now man various chapters set up throughout the country, and individual families can now sponsor a family through their cyber-sponsorship program. Though food is one of the biggest needs, staples also include coats, blankets, shoes, and personal care items. For more information, go to Family-to-Family.org.

A portion of this book's proceeds will benefit Family-to-Family!

Table of Contents

Introduction

"One of the very nicest things about life is the way we must regularly stop whatever it is we are doing and devote our attention to eating."

—Luciano Pavarotti and William Wright, from *Pavarotti, My Own Story*

What does dinner look like in your family?

Is there a disconnect between what it is and what you'd like it to be?

If so, join the club. If you're anything like me, you're lucky you can put your shirt on without the tag facing inside out, locate two socks that actually match, let alone find time to go to the grocery store and leave with everything on your list. Because of our crazy multi-tasking lives, dinner as we know it—or knew it—isn't as Rockwell-esque as the old days when Clair Huxtable or Carol Brady set a platter of chicken and mashed potatoes in front of a hungry group of kids and everyone talked and shared news about their days. (Yes, it was fiction, but it was based in truth.)

Somewhere between the countless soccer games, after school activities, tai kwan do, ballet lessons, sports clubs, tutors, and our 9-to-5 (or 6 or 7 jobs), we lost our way via take-out, order-in, drive-through and pick-up. Not that there's anything wrong with that, but... there is an old-fashioned fuzzy feeling within us (aka our guts) that reminds us we can do better.

You don't have to be a SuperMom to get dinner on the table. You just have to plan to plan.

Which is where this book enters stage right, flaunting a kitschy apron and a frying pan. You might not think it's possible... but you *can* get dinner on the table at least more than you're doing now. If you've read the statistics regarding families and the importance of family meals (more about that in Chapter One), you know that's a good thing.

This is not a recipe book, but a strategy book filled with ingredients for getting your family back to the dinner table.

It's also about finding your sanity (along with the salt and pepper)

My goal is simple: To help you plan, prep, cook ahead, freeze, embrace leftovers, and enjoy take-out—whatever it takes to get your family eating together, minus the electronics (and that includes hubby turning off his Blackberry or iPhone), without you falling on your face from exhaustion. It's meant to help solve that "Yikes!" feeling of realizing it's 6 p.m., and you're once again staring at your fridge, hoping a well-balanced dinner will suddenly pop out and set itself on the table. You're Mom: You're supposed to pull magic out of your hat, right? But in reality, you're beyond busy, acting as chauffeur, teacher, housekeeper, nurse, psychologist, entertainer, and disciplinarian, and too often have put dinner on the back burner (no pun intended). You need strategies. You need streamlining. And you need sanity. I know because I'm right there with you. And though it took me years to finally enjoy the preparation and planning of meals (and have embraced my microwave and frozen foods for this very reason), I've also missed the warmth, laughter, and camaraderie of sitting down as a family and connecting.

The strategies outlined in this book are meant to help you fill that gap not only with decent dinners (It's not a cookbook!), but with what fills your soul. Because, in the end, it's not about what you're serving that matters: It's that you're sitting together in the first place. Simple as it sounds, kids learn by example. Just by being with you, watching you, listening to you, and talking to you, they absorb good table manners, healthy eating habits, and the importance of conversation.

Reminder: This book is not about making you feel guilty. It's not about complicated recipes meant to turn you into Martha Stewart. Nor is it meant to berate you if you serve pizza, chicken nuggets, or Chinese take-out on occasion. Rather, it's meant to help you get your family to the table, turn off the TV, spark conversation, and spend quality time together. It's about taking the mayhem out of mealtime, solving your dinnertime dilemmas, and offering tips for reconnecting with your family.

This Book Is By Moms, For Moms

So you know: I'm not a nutritionist, dietician, or pediatrician. I'm a mom just like you. I'm also a writer, which got me interested in the subject in the first place. (I'm great about writing about other people's trials and tribulations but eventually put the microscope on myself.) My background includes a 20+ year career as a freelancer and editor at various women's magazines including *Woman's Day, Ladies' Home Journal, Woman's World, Women's Health & Fitness, Parents, Pregnancy, Good Housekeeping, BaBY,* and *InTown: Westchester.* My job has always been to interview a cadre of experts on various topics, and then cull down that research into an understandable and informative article.

Over the years I've become a "mini" expert on everything from sibling rivalry to birth order to traveling with kids. But the heart and soul of whatever I'm working on has always been other women: The people who are living and breathing specific situations and looking for reasonable, realistic solutions. After all, we're the ones on the front lines of knowing who best to call for what, or how to serve a halfway nutritious (no-fuss) meal. Think about it: How many times do you ask a friend for a recipe that you tasted at her house vs. pulling one from a magazine?

No offense to my former colleagues, but I've always been intimidated by those gorgeous looking roast chickens (often shellacked with hair spray for that page-ready photograph) and promises of "not your standard stew," when in fact, the ingredient list alone would keep me in the grocery store for close to an hour. It's all too perfect and pie-in-the-sky. It's my friends who give me the information I need to know: Other women like me who have demanding lives and are looking for simple solutions so they can go to bed at a decent hour.

Because most of the ideas in this book come from moms like you, they're honest. And, more important, *real*. I'm the first to admit I'm no Betty Crocker. Nor have I ever had any interest in cooking. But I *do* want to slow down and have at least one hour a day with my family, chatting over pasta, catching up over hamburgers, swapping ideas over chicken, and having my daughters know they have my and my husband's undivided attention through every stage of their lives.

1

I Don't Do Dinner

There's a sign on my fridge that reads, "I serve three meals: microwave, frozen and take-out" and, sadly, I'm not **exaggerating.** For me, the hardest part of the day is suppertime. The very question, "Mom, what's for dinner?" (usually before I've taken off my coat and walked in the door from work) is like fingernails on a chalkboard. *Who has time?*

In reality, dinner is a constant challenge, and I'm not embarrassed to admit that, over the years, I've served more than my share of less-than-ideal meals. In fact, my girls (now 14 and 17) like to tell the story of how, a few years ago, they called our local diner to get dinner delivered but were told, shortly after recounting their order, that they didn't have the $20 minimum required for delivery. So they said "thanks anyway" and hung up. But because of 21st century technology and caller ID, the manager of the diner called back. "Are you girls sure you don't want to order something else?" he asked, clearly concerned for their welfare. . . like the poor kids would go starving because

Did you know?

The average American eats six convenience foods daily.

their mom hadn't prepared dinner for them. (The truth is I *did* have some chicken cutlets in the freezer and was on my way home with groceries.) The fact that we didn't sit down for dinner as a family that night or the other nights that followed was just icing on the cake.

Why couldn't I get it together like other women I know?

It wasn't always this way. Depending on my various stages of "momhood:" new mom, working part-time, working-full-time-with-long-commute, working-from-home, commuting-again (though closer to home)—you get the gist—we've had various stages of *dinner*. There was us all eating together, which involved me trying to juggle a bottle into Kid Number Two while spoon feeding mashed potatoes to Kid Number One, while also managing to occasionally grab bites of steak with my fingers. Then there was me serving something simple, like elbow macaroni (with various sauces for everyone), with me up and down a million times because one kid's pasta wasn't hot enough, another decides she hates pasta, wants chicken nuggets ... then ketchup ... then juice ... then me forgetting the garlic bread burning in the oven for the meal my husband and I were eating. Not to mention in between this dinner dance, my husband and I trying to have a conversation about something other than poopy diapers, before we have to get up from the table to change said diapers or clean up a juice spill before someone starts crying/ whining/screaming (select your loud sound), then throwing pasta on the floor. Which then turns into (select one of the following): Temper tantrum, food fights, bad manners, burping, vomiting, spitting, kicking and, eventually, a Sesame Street video (or some *Baby Einstein* tape—after all, we all want our kids to be brilliant)... all of which buys me (us? Did my husband leave the room?) the five minutes of peace needed so I can indulge in a now tepid glass of Chardonnay.

Pick an exasperated word, any exasperated word. Is it any wonder, that after all that commotion, I switched from having us all eat together to attending to everyone in shifts, first feeding my kids, and then making a separate meal for my husband. (Hello ten pounds of weight gain as I ate their leftovers to tide myself over while waiting for darling hubby.)

How Did Things Change So Much?

What a difference a few generations makes. Growing up, I had the experience of sitting at the dinner table every night, my dad commanding one end of our Formica® table, my mom on the other, and my sister and I facing each other. There was no TV in sight. A hot home-cooked casserole was served in a Pyrex® dish in the middle, complete with steam rising from a plate of creamed corn. We had placemats and sometimes even cloth napkins. Dishes were passed with "please" and "thank you." My parents would ask about our days. And my sister, Ann, and I would actually (politely) recount them.

Despite the rose-colored nostalgia I'm painting, and despite the fact that I did occasionally kick my sister under the table and pour soda into her mashed potatoes when she wasn't looking, we knew the family dinner hour was more or less sacrosanct.

Fast forward to today, where rounding up the troops is often a logistical nightmare, with meals a catch-as-catch-can proposition, grabbed on the run, often in recyclable containers or grease-soaked paper bags, eaten between traffic lights on the way to or from this practice, that lesson, or this meeting. We eat standing up at

Kids will challenge you with their tantrums and picky eating habits, but stick to your mission of having them join you at the dinner table.

Fact

Research shows that only 43% of homemade dinners served in the U.S. include vegetables.

the counter, on the way from the stove to the table, or from the table back to the sink. Pick a place, any place: On the floor, in front of the TV, on the sofa, at our kitchen islands. Invariably we gobble our meals, hurried, dipping, dunking, slurping, sipping, but rarely *enjoying* as one at the kitchen table.

I'm not alone. Often, when I call my girlfriends at around 6 or 7 p.m. and say, "Am I calling at a bad time? Are you eating dinner?" they sound just like me: "Nope, we all grabbed a slice between soccer practice," or "The kids ate, but I'm waiting for Bruce," or "Dinner? Is that what you call me eating a frozen Lean Cuisine® and the kids gobbling down Hot Pockets®?"

And I haven't even talked about incorporating the Holy Grail known as the food pyramid. For years, my eldest only ate hot dogs, while my youngest vacillated between pizza and chicken nuggets. Hardly a balanced meal. In fact, we joked in our house that a balanced meal meant sitting on the kitchen chairs without falling. Thinking about a starch, a vegetable, a fruit, a fiber, and an entrée is hard enough when you need a huge calendar/GPS navigational device to track every person's whereabouts.

The pressure-cooker that is parenthood means the family dinner has virtually disappeared. Today, less than half of American families eat dinner together—despite the fact that 98 percent of moms say it's important. And when they do, most meals last less than 20 minutes and are often lacking in proper nutrition.

While we can't help but think about "the old days" with Mom at the stove cooking for us all day, our lives have changed. Yes, there's a certain amount of nostalgia in play here, but (and BUT!), there's also our 21st century reality: We need to create a new kind of family meal.

The Reasons to Get Back to the Table

And so, the question becomes: *Does it really matter whether we all eat dinner together?* The answer, say experts, is a spoon–banging *yes*. Study after study proves time spent gathered at the kitchen table is a significant way to strengthen family bonds. Counted among the benefits are higher quality of food, better nutrition, and portion control, as well as emotional nurturing, sense of belonging, better grades, less delinquency, and overall family unity, not to mention cost savings (less ordering in and eating out).

In case you haven't heard the sobering statistics, here are a few:

* Fewer than one-third of all children eat dinner with both parents on any given night.

* Teens from families that almost never eat dinner together are 72 percent more likely to use illegal drugs, cigarettes, and alcohol than the average teen. They are also more likely to have lower grades, higher rates of addiction, poor eating habits, and a higher risk of depression and eating disorders.

* Researchers from the National Center on Addiction and Substance Abuse (CASA) at

Stats to Know:

- The average family spends more than $2,000 per year on dinners away from home, with 10% of those dinners coming from McDonalds.

- More than half of the dinners eaten by overweight American children are consumed in front of the television.

- Meals eaten with family have about 50% more fruits and vegetables than meals consumed alone.

- Family meals are three times more likely to include low-fat choices.

SOURCE: BUREAU OF LABOR

It's proven: Time spent gathered at the kitchen table strengthens family bonds.

10 Benefits of Family Dinners

1. Everyone eats healthier meals.
2. Kids are less likely to become overweight or obese.
3. Kids are more likely to stay away from cigarettes.
4. Teens are less likely to drink alcohol.
5. Teens are less likely to try marijuana and other drugs.
6. School grades will be better.
7. You and your children will talk more.
8. You'll be more likely to hear about a serious problem.
9. Kids will feel like you're proud of them.
10. There will be less stress and tension at home.

Columbia University found that the less often a family eats together, the worse the experience is likely to be, the less nutritional the food, and the more mundane the dialogue, if any at all. Among those who eat together three or fewer times a week, 45 percent say they eat with the TV on (as opposed to 37 percent of all households), with nearly one-third admitting there is little to no conversation. Parents with less than a high school education share more meals with their kids than do parents with high school diplomas or college degrees.

* A majority of teens who ate three or fewer meals a week with their families wished they did so more often.

The kitchen table (where I've written half this book, in fact) is everything: It's the Grand Central Station of our homes, where good news is celebrated with clinks of champagne glasses, homework is scribbled and erased over the knobby pines of a scratched table, holiday kids' tables are set until way past a child still belongs at said table, and heated discussions take place long into the night over mugs of hot coffee. It's the hearth of the home, the centerpiece of our togetherness. It's where we gossip with friends, chat with a neighbor over freshly baked banana bread, or set out our graveyard of ruined recipes to prove to our husbands that yes, we really did spend the day cooking.

The dinner hour takes over the kitchen like no other meal: It's the nightcap to a long six hours we've all been apart, the smell of what's cooking in the oven (or heated up in the microwave), the warm embrace we need at the end of a long day. It's here where we catch up and, hopefully, slow down.

Having this block of time set aside to communicate allows us to stay updated on our kids' school and social lives. It's where children's vocabularies are broadened from listening to our conversations. Not to mention the big bonus: When you include kids in discussions, they feel valued, that we're interested in what they have to say.

Being together and mingling over meals teaches your kids other important skills, too, such as sharing ("Please pass the bread."), compromise ("Johnny is taking the bread right now, you'll have to wait."), negotiation, ("If I pass you the peas, will you pass me the salad?"), learning when to interrupt ("Someone left the stove on!") and when not to inter-

Mom Tips

"I highly recommend talking to kids about foods they enjoy and foods that they would like to taste. By bringing them with me to the farmer's market, we learn about, and taste, new ingredients that get them excited. Then, we watch the Food Network, flip through cookbooks, and browse online for recipes that sound delicious. If you want to have them help you cook, have all of the ingredients ready in advance. Otherwise, they will lose interest too quickly to get anything productive done."
—Michelle Stern, San Rafael, CA, mom of two, ages 7 and 9, and owner of What's Cooking

"As both a therapist and a parent, it's what happens around the table—social interactions, conversation, sharing, nurturing, and nourishing—that seem important. I don't think it matters much which meal it is, but rather the quality of the time spent together."
— Liz Sawyer Danowski, Oxford, England, mom of one son, age 5

Did you know?

More than one in five parents say they are simply "too busy" to have family dinners together. The most common reason teenagers give as to why family dinners are not more frequent is that "parents work late." The most common reason parents give is "conflicting schedules."

SOURCE: NATIONAL CENTER ON ADDIC-
TION AND SUBSTANCE ABUSE (CASA) AT
COLUMBIA UNIVERSITY

rupt ("When is it my turn to talk?"), as well as learning manners ("May I be excused?"), in addition to teamwork ("Please help bring the plates to the sink") and problem solving, ("I thought I put four forks on the table"). All translate to lifelong interpersonal and communication skills.

The benefits far outweigh our "we're too busy" excuses:

✔ **You'll eat more healthfully.** And so will your kids. Youngsters left to themselves often opt for a junk food diet of chips, pastries and processed foods, and, often a lifetime of bad habits. Young people who regularly eat meals with their families eat more fruit, vegetables, whole grains, and calcium-rich foods, and drink fewer soft drinks than other people their age, according to a five-year study from the University of Minnesota. Plus, portion sizes will be more appropriate at home, cutting down on extra calories and fat. Food made at home tends to be eaten in smaller quantities. A study by Harvard Medical School reports that chances of being overweight are 15 percent lower among those who eat dinner with their family "most days" or "every day." Not only is a set meal time a chance to encourage your children to make healthy nutritional choices, but also an opportunity to help them make healthy lifestyle decisions.

✔ **You'll become more conscious of how you are eating.** Family meals (sans TV) encourage slow eating as opposed to a grab-and-go meal. According to ex-

One of the benefits of the family meal is that kids do better in school.

perts, it takes 20 minutes for your stomach to tell your brain it's full. In a fast-food generation, we don't always wait those 20 minutes. Taking the time to eat more slowly can mean fewer calories taken in.

✔ **You'll be a better communicator.** Mealtime conversations have been shown to improve young people's vocabulary, according to studies by the University of Minnesota. Chatting with your family about your town's green policies or the latest blockbuster movie has the hidden benefit of improving your conversational and thinking skills.

✔ **Your kids will do better in school.** A study of first graders' reading readiness found that "high scorers had a radically different atmosphere around the meal table," as compared to the low scorers. The former group enjoyed family meals that were "a focus for total family interaction." Another study proves teens reported earning more As and Bs in school than students who ate dinner with their families fewer than three times a week.

Surprise fact:

Why aren't parents and kids eating together? "interference of teen activities" and "television watching that simply cannot be missed."

SOURCE: NATIONAL CENTER ON ADDICTION AND SUBSTANCE ABUSE (CASA) AT COLUMBIA UNIVERSITY

✔ **You're doing your teens a favor.** Teens who eat with their families five or more times per week are less likely to abuse drugs, alcohol, and tobacco, according to CASA. If you have a girl, you're also preventing her from developing an eating disorder. Teen girls sharing at least five or more family meals per week were less likely to use diet pills or laxatives, binge eat, or vomit to control their weight, according to the Minnesota researchers.

✔ **You'll save money.** The Bureau of Labor Statistics reports that the average American family spends more than $2,000 per year on dinners outside the home.

✔ **You'll be happier.** Mealtimes create memories and bring families closer, with many folks reporting a larger sense of unity, love, self-confidence, and understanding, all of which is fostered around the dinner table. And surprise, surprise: The majority of teens in a study by CASA—84 percent—report they actually want to eat dinner with their families.

Why This Book Is For You

Most likely, I'm not telling you anything you don't know. It doesn't take a rocket scientist to know that walking into a home where the aroma of a bubbling stew or a hot-out-of-the-oven lasagna tickles your nose will make you feel comforted, welcomed, and warm. What you *don't* know—and what I didn't know either, until I started doing some research—is that it's possible to get into a family meal groove, even if you haven't done it for years. It's just a matter of simple tactics.

Doing Dinner Better

Of course, as with most things, getting started is the hardest part. In my case, it was a sharp kick in the pants, otherwise known as The Guilt Trip, that got me going. It wasn't long after "the diner episode" that I began to realize I needed to change our two-meals-a-night policy, separating my husband and me from our children. Truthfully, I was tired of being a short-order cook and trying to please everyone. I was also angry at myself for always eating my kids' leftovers as a way to tide myself over until my husband came home. (I was also secretly glad Diner Guy didn't call Social Services on me.)

The whole "I should be doing dinner better" thing came to a head after we visited my sister at her California home. My sister always enjoyed cooking (not me; I burn toast), so when she had kids, she didn't stop her gourmet adventures. Her daughter, Arin began eating fish—at age six. And her daughter, Lily, ate salad at the unheard of age of two. They all eat together every night, despite the fact that her husband is a doctor who tends to work insane hours. But when my then nine-year-old started counting down the days on her calendar to when we'd visit my sister, I realized I needed to step up to the plate. "Dinner at Auntie Ann's is one of the best parts of visiting," she told me when I inquired about the calendar countdown markings. "Because, unlike us, they all eat together."

Yes, kids say the darndest things. But they also say the most honest things. And so, a few years ago, I started planning meals that I felt the whole family could and should eat. I consulted friends (and, of course, my sister), read countless blogs, talked to experts, researched books, and started shopping more strategically to make dinnertime less stressful. And though I'm in no way perfect, and clearly no Rachael Ray,

Invite extended family and friends over for dinner as a way to get everyone talking.

I did come up with some creative and fresh ways to bring back dinner—everything from proclaiming taco night, to upside-down day (breakfast for dinner), to promoting sandwiches and wraps to dinner status.

There Are Many Ways to Do This

Sure, some of us get lucky. We like to cook. Or our husbands like to cook. Or our kids like to eat. Or we live next door to a Trader Joe's (that—in our dreams—delivers). But others of us need help. In fact *most* of us need help. When I began interviewing moms about their experiences, I was thrilled to learn they shared my views (and yes, dread). I heard things like "Even Hamburger Helper takes too long," or "I'd rather sleep than cook," or "My son hates everything," or "I'd seriously stop buying clothes for a year if my husband would let me hire a personal chef."

Other women don't see the point of family meals because they either grew up without them or grew up with unpleasant memories, and so don't have that nostalgic frame of reference. For them, the ritual of family meals is a learning process of giving to their kids what they never had, but what they realize now is a valuable way to bond.

Whatever your situation, this book is meant to offer a hodgepodge of strategies, ideas, and suggestions meant to ease the witching hour when toddlers hang on us, colicky babies need to be soothed, school-age children need to be chauffeured, and dinner becomes one more thing to do on a never-ending list of to-dos.

Dinner FYI

It's 6 p.m. . . Do you know where your dinner is? Go to casafamilyday.org, a national initiative launched by CASA, for information and activities.

Starting Today, Let This Book Be Your Guide.

Set aside mealtime for meals—nothing else. Granted, it will take time. And it will take patience. And it will take practice. And it won't always work out. But make it a goal. You wouldn't have picked up this book if you didn't think you needed to do better than what you're doing now. But as my kids have gotten older, and our lives have gotten busier, I've realized how important that time really is.

Lest you think I'm getting all cliché and just plain corny, let me say first and foremost that I'm all about making your life easier.

Get your kids involved in the kitchen.

We're all different. There is no one-size-fits-all solution. The strategies outlined in the following chapters are meant to be treated the way you'd look at an *a la carte* menu: You can choose what you like and skip what you don't. After all, we have our own parenting styles, hectic schedules, picky eaters, and house rules. Some of us can be neurotic about organization, want to wear an apron, and cook from scratch, while others of us just want to know how to dress up a can of soup. From the quote I gave you in the beginning of this chapter, you can tell I fall into the latter category. And while I've graduated to freezer and batch cooking (on occasion), I'm still a huge proponent of prepared foods and order-in Chinese.

What I've learned from countless conversations with moms and experts is this: It doesn't really matter what you cook (or don't cook) for dinner. What you're really offering is a hefty serving of comfort: A time out from our busy, overscheduled lives to wind down, turn off the electronic devices, tune in to each other, and set in motion a ritual your kids will long remember and hopefully pass on to their children.

2

Ready. . . Set. . . Go!

Some women dream of designer jeans, Botox, beach houses, and lavish vacations. I, instead, pine for a personal chef. Someone who will plan and cook every family meal, make them nutritious and enticing to my kids, serve, chop, clean up, and unload the dishwasher.

We moms just don't seem to have enough hours in the day. We're shuttling our kids to play dates, soccer games, tutors, or piano lessons. We're trying to get them to play nicely, use the potty, clean up their toys, or not kick the back of our seats while we're driving to do our millions of errands. We're throwing in laundry, balancing our checkbooks, making the beds, filling out back-to-school forms, parting their hair, and vacuuming cookie crumbs. We're trying to juggle a career, keep the house in order and, oh yeah, spend *quality time* with our kids and our husbands and, if we're lucky, still have a piece of ourselves left over at the end of the day.

Eating dinner together twice a week is better than nothing at all.

Where Is a Sit-Down Dinner Supposed to Fit In?

It's a question that comes up in many mom conversations. Do a Google search, and you'll find hundreds of online articles and blogs discussing the craziness of the dinner hour. No doubt, as you read this, one mom somewhere is ordering Chinese take-out while another is boiling a pot for her standby mac and cheese. And while there's nothing wrong with any of that—this book is meant to give you strategies, not make you feel guilty for serving something easy and out of the box—there is something to be said for slowing down and making mealtimes a priority.

In a perfect world, I'd love to sit down with my family to a home-cooked meal seven nights a week. But let's be honest: Life isn't perfect. From where I sit, managing motherhood, career, husband, girlfriends, the dog, the house, the extended family, etc., it just seems to get more challenging. In this time-pressed age, when both parents in many families work full-time, and children race from sports practices to piano lessons until well past 6 p.m., dinner is a "time-suck" that occurs at the witching hour, that lull between the end of the day and the beginning of the evening. If you have young children, it's often their melt-down time after long days of play dates, daycare, or missed naps. For older kids, it's a quick peek at whatever's in the fridge before rushing off to ballet or baseball, or diving into mounds of homework. And for us frazzled moms with a slew of balls in the air, it's the time when everything comes to a head. We're tired. We're hungry. They're tired.

They're hungry. And most likely we're also out of bread/milk/eggs/fill in the blank, or we just realized that we don't have that primo ingredient necessary for whipping up our last-minute standby. No doubt, if most of us could wave our magic wands, we'd wish the dinner fairy would set a steaming plate of home-cooked, nutritious food in front of all of us.

But since none of this is happening anytime soon (though a gal can dream), we need to figure out a way to make it easier, to streamline our days so that the dinner load doesn't come crashing down on us with a thud of guilt and angst. Again, I'm not talking about getting a home-cooked meal on the table every night. If you can manage seven nights a week, more power to you. But if it's only one or two nights a week, then that's fine too.

Set a Goal and Build On That

Figure out your shortcomings. If it's the main course you get stuck on, then buy a rotisserie chicken, and cook the side dishes. If it's prepping the vegetables that bogs you down, buy frozen, or pre-cut items. If it's all of the above, fortify an ordered-in pizza with pre-cut broccoli or ready-made chicken. And for goodness sake, allow yourself some breathing room. Don't apologize for store-bought pre-cut *anything* or the occasional frozen meal.

✔ **Keep Your Expectations Realistic.** Take this dinner thing in baby steps. Parenting coach Julie Freedman Smith, a mom of two from Calgary, Canada, references this line from Lisa Martin, author of

> ### Mom Tip
>
> *"I actually cook dinner at 10 or 11 p.m. for the next night while I'm blogging. That way, if something takes 30 minutes, at least I'm working in between [getting things into] the oven. Or, for example, while I'm making breakfast, I'll throw the grain/rice on the stove for that night; then while I'm making lunch, I'll do the vegetables, etc. That way by the end of the day, the meal's cooked."*
> —Nicole Bohorad, North Bergen, NJ, mom of one, 21 months
>
> *"Always keep a clutter-free table. This will be one less thing you have to do when the time comes for dinner. A clean table screams, 'Eat at me!'"*
> —Dawn Billesbach, Thorton, CO, mom of two, ages 5 and 7, creator of MenuFortheWeek.com
>
> *"The number-one rule in my house is no TV at dinner time. I am starting this early since my son is not yet two, but if your kids never watch TV during dinner they won't miss it."*
> —Kameron Scampoli, Providence, RI, mom of an infant and a 2-year-old

Don't be embarrassed about buying chicken and sides from the grocery store salad bar.

©ISTOCKPHOTO.COM/MONKEYBUSINESSIMAGES

Briefcase Moms: Guilt is the difference between reality and expectations. In other words, when we have high expectations for ourselves and don't meet them, we tend to feel guilty, which leads us into thinking we're bad moms. But if we lower our expectations, we don't feel as bad. The lesson here: Do not do everything at once. Make small changes, and do so within the realm of what works for your family and your lifestyle. This getting around the dinner table may only happen once a week or twice a month, but at least it's more than you were doing before. Whatever you do, don't compare yourself to Susie down the street or anyone else. Work with your reality.

✔ **Plan To Plan.** Practicality is key. Even after spending nearly a year working on this book, I'm still trying to practice what I preach and plan what I can ahead of time, be it my grocery list or plotting out my family's calendar. And, yes, my husband and two daughters have gotten better at coming together at mealtimes, gradually transitioning from our set-in-stone Sunday night ritual to four weekday nights *most* of the time. I've also gotten smarter about preparing foods, stocking my pantry, and shopping with a plan so I'm not going to the food store every day or even twice a day—something I often did. I now, proudly, go once or twice a week.

✔ **Set Aside Two to Three Hours a Week.** If you're really committed to getting your family to the dinner table together, then you need to create that space in your life. Set aside the time to cook, shop, and plan. It will be so much easier than trying to do it on the fly. Marked on your calendar with just as much importance as other things in your life, dinner will soon become much more manageable and enjoyable. Put another way: You can't put new goals on an old template. If you truly want to make dinner a priority, you have to change your ways.

✓ **Decide On Your Grocery Days and Your Family Nights.** Make the days you shop become a routine so everyone knows Mom's going to the store on Sunday. Need anything? No excuses! The more you set to a routine, say 10 a.m. every Sunday, the easier it will become part of your everyday rhythm. Same with setting up your family's dinner plans. Maybe it's every Sunday and Friday, or every Monday and Wednesday. Set this plan in stone—what you can within reason—and stick to it so it becomes something you all expect. I hate to admit it, but I'm often better at my job and sticking to my work deadlines than I am with my own family's needs. I can't tell you how many times I've switched my

When all else fails . . .

. . . you can find something that you can prepare in less than five minutes: There's always grilled cheese, or a peanut butter sandwich, or scrambled eggs, or cereal.

Mom Tip

"Plan a routine, and then plan to be flexible enough to resort to peanut butter and jelly, graham crackers, yogurt, cereal, or leftovers, to get you through those times when your plans need to be reworked."
—Diane Asyre, St. Louis, MO, mom of three, ages 10, 12, and 13

Mom Tip

"The best way to save at the grocery store is to become a price expert. Read the grocery store inserts and learn the market prices. I buy chicken breasts, beef, and pork at lowest market prices and freeze them in individually wrapped packages. I have price points at which I purchase each type of meat; e.g. don't pay more than $1.77/lb. for boneless, skinless chicken breasts ever. When it goes on sale I buy at least eight pounds. That usually lasts until the next sale."

—Shay Pausa, Scottsdale, AZ, mom of two, ages 7 and 10

"My biggest food tip for moms is to know how to put together three or four basic meals based primarily on pantry staples. That might mean pasta with veggies and/or beans, a frittata, or a stir-fry. These become go-to recipes that moms can vary based on the specifics of what they have on-hand."

—Jenna Helwig, Brooklyn, NY, mom of one, age 4, RoseBerry.com

kids' doctors appointments because I had something to do for my job, or how many times I figured I could stock up on items at the grocery store another day because I had errands to run. I'm all about flexibility, but there is something to be said for setting up a routine and sticking to it as best you can. You end up accomplishing more, and that feels good.

✔ **Stick To Your Guns.** Don't let one or two cancellations to your new and improved schedule discourage you. If family meal time doesn't work out one week, try for two times the following week. Or make your together time an after-school snack, late-night dessert, or Sunday brunch until you can get back on track. Be flexible within reason, but also try and figure out ways for it to work. Regular rhythms make it much easier to keep your routine going over time. Allow family members some free passes, but make sure they understand the consequences of missing a dinner together. In other words: *No free passes the next time*, no matter what.

✔ **Get Your Family to Pitch In** It's not about cooking (though we have easy fool-proof recipes at the end of this book). It's more about getting everyone to the table. If your family doesn't like what you're serving, hand them a cookbook, and tell them to whip up whatever they'd like instead (something my sister did when she was about 11 after complaining to my mother, so she became our cook one night a week). Kids *can*

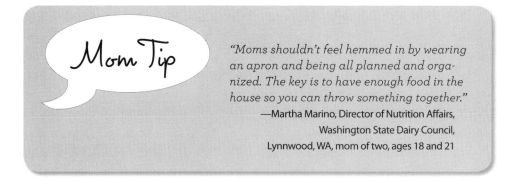

Mom Tip

"Moms shouldn't feel hemmed in by wearing an apron and being all planned and organized. The key is to have enough food in the house so you can throw something together."
—Martha Marino, Director of Nutrition Affairs, Washington State Dairy Council, Lynnwood, WA, mom of two, ages 18 and 21

cook. There are plenty of cookbooks out there that cater to them. You just have to be there to supervise.

I also encourage you to make grocery shopping a family affair. If your kids don't like what you're serving, take them to the supermarket, and have them select a few items they do like. That way, if they complain about what's for dinner, reach into the fridge and remind them that they made these choices.

✔ **Get Your Family On Board Early** From where I sit (often on the edge of a kitchen stool, if I sit at all) we moms are way too accommodating to our families, often acting as short-order cooks, serving each child something different, and still something else for our hubby during a later shift. It's enough already. We need a better plan.

✔ **It's Never Too Late** Part of the reason many families don't eat together is that parents find it easier to eat without the kids. You *can* change your ways. You can compromise. It's a process. Do I wish I started earlier? Yes. Do I wish I had been able to do it more? Definitely. But it's never too late, despite the initial resistance you may get. Remember, in the end, it doesn't matter if your little one whines in his high chair or that you serve macaroni and cheese *again*, what matters is that you got everyone together.

Here's a secret: I didn't really do this myself until my oldest was in middle school. When my girls were younger, it just didn't make sense to have them wait until my husband came home from work. They were tired and cranky—and so was I. So I'd feed them first, often in front of the TV, while I prepared a *real* dinner for my husband and me. That same situation continued—we were used to it after all—as they moved from preschool to grade school. Even though they could have feasibly stayed up to wait for Mark, we were stuck in our routine with homework and after school activities. It took a few years of rushing, trying to feed everyone different meals at different times, and *still* everyone complaining there was nothing to eat in the fridge, that I realized there had to be a better way.

My husband and I grew up eating with our parents. We knew the value, so we shifted gears. And we told our kids what the new rules would be. It wasn't until much later into their high school years that they started to rebel against us. (But this is fodder for another book entirely.)

Hopefully you're at the other end of the spectrum. You have a toddler who's just transitioned to finger foods or a kindergartener who's learning the rules about being a "big girl or boy," and you realize that it's better to start sooner rather than later. You need to get your kids to the table as early as possible. It's not only a great motivator, but the lessons learned by sitting with you and interacting with other family members are invaluable.

How to Survive (and Enjoy) The Dinner Hour

Think of the following strategies as an *a la carte* menu. Take a little bit of one strategy or two of another. The key is to be gradual about it. And if something doesn't work one week, don't be hard on yourself. Just try it again the following week. Or modify your experience. Ask your family for input and suggestions. Involve them.

Fresh or Frozen?

Sometimes frozen fruits and vegetables are more nutritious than fresh. The longer fruits or vegetables sit around waiting to be sold or eaten, the more nutrients they lose. But fruits and vegetables grown for freezing are usually frozen right after they're picked. Therefore, they have less time to lose their nutrients.

Bottom line: Fresh is best, frozen is a close second and canned is only for adding to soups or if on a tight budget. Canned foods, especially veggies, have tons of sodium.

©BIGSTOCKPHOTO.COM/IFONG

And make it fun. One mom I know has an assigned dinner night when each member of the family gets to choose the meal of the night. Another has her grade school kids create the ambiance of a restaurant at home. The kids write up a menu and help mom make something they like to order when they eat out. Chicken fingers count, as does spaghetti. Simple touches like adding fancier napkins, nice plates (china, if your kids won't break them), some flowers and candles, and moving dinner to the dining room can change the mood drastically.

Remember, this is about getting your children back into the "old-world" tradition of sitting down, slowing down, and conversing over food. As one mom told me, "Dinner is only a 'crazy hour' when your lifestyle is focused on everything *but* sitting down to dinner with your family. The key is to make dinner the priority, not the afterthought."

Here is Your Smorgasbord of Ideas

The following menu of options and opinions comes from many months of talking to moms just like you: Working moms, stay-at-home-moms, harried moms, calm moms, moms of those with one child, moms of those with more (think 14: Hello Shannah Godfrey of Independence, Missouri), "foodie" moms (check out Jennifer Perillo at InJenniesKitchen.com; we feature a recipe from her on page 193), blogging moms, frugal moms (shout out to Jenn Fowler at FrugalUpstate.com), moms who grow their own gardens, organic moms (see my new pal Amanda Louden at EatYourRoots.org),

Try The 2/3 Rule

It's a given: Most families have kids with different tastes. Heck, it's rare that my husband and I always agree. I could eat pasta every night, he could eat chicken. So since no one in their right mind wants to prepare a different meal for each family member, you should aim for something that gives options. In other words, The 2/3 Rule: A little bit of something for everyone. Just put out veggies, fruit, or potatoes family-style in the middle of the table, with a protein on the side, and let everyone dig in. Giving options will make you less crazy (the ultimate goal) and make your children and hubby feel that you are at least trying to accommodate their various needs and tastes. There are so many choices today at the grocery store, with pre-cut meat and veggies or store-bought rotisserie chicken, that can make your table look nice—and filled with plenty for everyone—even if you haven't done more than simply set the table.

"Why do I love my freezer? Let me count the ways:

1. *I can stockpile meat and seafood.*

2. *I can make extra stocks, soups, sauces and casseroles for use on a busy day.*

3. *Even bits of extra bananas, strawberries, and other fruits and berries can be squirreled away for a future smoothie rather than letting them spoil.*

4. *Breads, muffins, and simple cakes can be stored."*

—Laurie Zerga, Alameda, CA, mom of two, ages 19 and 21, Chef-K.com.

• •

"I'm big into planning 'something easy' nights, which means I've prepped ahead of time. Chili, stews, and chicken all freeze well. I fill a quart-size freezer bag with two servings and freeze them flat. They will defrost in 10 minutes in a sink of warm water. I can usually make about four meals at a time this way, and keep a variety of prepped meals in the freezer."

—Chris Ann Sepkowski, Mamaroneck, NY, mom/stepmom of six kids, ages 4 to 24

moms (like me) who burn toast, moms who batch-cook (go to OnceAMonthMom.com), moms who empower you to cook (MealMakeoverMoms.com), and moms who own cooking schools (go to BeansproutsCafe.com) and are good at sneaking veggies in their kid's meals.

I also spoke to many mom-experts whose advice—both professional and personal—proved invaluable. Martha Marino, the Director of Nutrition Affairs Communications at the Lynnwood, Washington-based Washington State Dairy Council shared her up-to-date research, educational resources, as well her files of information and quotes from those she's lectured to over the years (check out the coffee smoothie recipe she gave me on page 163 and go to EatSmart.org). She also gave me plenty of anecdotal stories about being a single mom to Matt and Julia, now young adults who share their mom's love of family meals.

A lot of information also comes from Denver nutritionist (and mom) Julie Hammerstein who works primarily with kids, families and single parents on how to navigate healthy eating and lifestyle habits. Her motto is "improving global nutrition one family at a time," and her suggestions for grocery shopping, meal planning, thinking ahead, and quick snack ideas, etc. are peppered throughout the book (go to her website at MaxLifeTherapies.com or Twitter.com/jhammerstein to see what she's up to). Another very impressive resource: Beth Oden, a Boulder, Colorado-based family nutrition coach and mom of two who offered a laundry list of creative strategies that had me experimenting on my kids the minute I hung up the phone with her (aNutritionMission.com).

I also relied heavily on feeding expert and

Write it down. Planning meals ahead of time is the key to success.

author Ellyn Satter (EllynSatter.com) and lifestyle coaches like Julie Freedman Smith of Parenting Power™ (ParentingPower.ca) of Calgary, Alberta and mom of two, ages 6 and 10, and Taiha Wagner of Eden Prairie, Minnesota (JustOneBite.net), who is a therapeutic lifestyle educator, and has three kids, ages 7, 11, and 16. Others, you'll hear from firsthand in the mom tips that accompany every chapter. After all: Doesn't mom know best? As I've gotten older, I've realized that despite our insecurities as women, one thing reads true: Trust your gut. Which is why I have confidence in what so many parents around the country told me, and why I think that they do have the recipe (pun intended) for success.

✔ **Pace yourself.** If you put too high an expectation on yourself, especially if you're someone like me who can barely get dinner on the table three nights a week, you'll set yourself up for failure. Be honest about what your family's demands are and what can be compromised to make sitting down together for a meal reasonably work. This is not the time to map out your menu planning for the week on an Excel sheet. Just plot out one dinner for one night and make it something manageable, even if that something is just soup and sandwiches. Start out realistically—maybe every Sunday evening—then work for more evenings. My family started with taco nights and went from there.

✔ **Make it a commitment.** Choose an easy night that works for you, like a Friday or Sunday, and commit yourself to making this a regular activity. By starting on a Friday, for example, you're setting the tone for bringing the family together for the weekend after the family has been scattered for the week. My family likes Sunday

Strategies for Dinner with Your Baby

Feed your baby first. Babies are unpredictable. And while it would be great if your little one could sit in a highchair between you and your hubby while you catch up on your day, that scenario is often not realistic. In the old days this is what my husband and I did. We'd feed our daughter, Corey, first, play with her, give her a bath, and put her to bed, with one of us taking bed/bath duty, the other making dinner. We'd then eat at 8:30 or 9 p.m. and get a chance to talk. Sometimes we even lit the candles and felt like we were dating all over again.

Feed your baby twice. If your baby is starting to eat table food, it's nice to have your child sit and partake in the evening meal. Children like to mimic, which is another reason why having your child there to copy your eating habits is a good idea. If you opt for this scenario, you're better off feeding your child a healthy snack like vegetables or pasta at 5 p.m. so she won't be cranky/hungry/crying when you and your husband are ready for dinner. You can then feed her something again when the two of you sit down, keeping the family meal intact.

Put the baby in the swing beside you. Eat. Push baby. Watch baby gurgle with happiness. Actually look at husband across table and smile. Life is grand. . . until your baby starts crying. At which point dinner is over. . . didn't you know that's why they invented microwaves—to warm up the rest of your dinner later?

Bottom line: You know your baby and his schedule/disposition. Do the best you can. And don't sweat it. At this point, it's really not necessary to have your infant at the dinner table with you.

nights for the opposite reason. It's a great way to start the week, plus Sundays tend to be lazier, and I'm less crazed and more organized.

✔ **Set a time.** Try to eat dinner at the same hour every night, figuring out the time of the evening when everyone will be around. Even if it's only 20 minutes, making this appointment with your family carves out time in everyone's crazy schedules to take a break. Keep to it as best you can while remaining reasonably flexible. It will take work, but it's doable, and the results will be worth it.

✔ **Pen it in.** Write it on your calendar or block time for it on your Blackberry. And make sure your husband is on the same page. If you have teenage kids they, too, must put this in red ink and know there are no ifs, ands, or buts. Other obligations should be scheduled around dinner, not the other way around. Including everyone in the family sends the message that the family is important (even the sulking teenagers).

Choose after-school activities carefully so that the dinner ritual is preserved most days of the week. It *can* be done. This helps your kids understand that dinner together is a priority.

Try to dine at the same time every night.

Tempting a Toddler's Tastebuds

- For young children, food is all about presentation. Make it look fun and inviting, or your child will not eat it. Melt cheese on top of broccoli, and pretend they are little trees. Cut peanut butter sandwiches into the shape of small bricks, and lay them on top of each other.

- Alter the shape of the food you're presenting. It might be served julienne-style, in round shapes, Asian-cut, grated, or in the shape of an animal. Cookie cutters help.

- Bribery works. Granted it's not politically correct, and the parenting experts reading this are most likely cringing at this statement. But as an imperfect mom, it's worked for me, and I don't think it's bad to do in small doses. I'm not talking anything expensive, but perhaps a sticker, an extra ten minutes of TV, another book at bedtime, etc., if they can sit at the table for five minutes longer or take another bite of something healthy.

- Have your kids participate in the food prep. That is usually a winner, as they feel proud of what they made and are more willing to eat it/try it.

- Involve them in the meal planning, i.e., going to farmers markets, or joining a CSA (see page 53): They always have a lot of kids' events.

- Start a garden, indoors or out. Kids love to eat what they can grow themselves.

- Tell funny stories, and keep the lines of communication open. This has the potential to distract kids while they are eating, and they end up eating what's on their plate without realizing it.

- Use fancy toothpicks (with caution). I used to roll up plain turkey, put a fancy toothpick on top, and my daughter, Sydney, would eat it up. Use the kind with decorations on top, not the colored ones, as the dye gets on the turkey and defeats your purpose. I also would use them for cut-up potatoes, string beans, and anything else on her plate. Just be careful she doesn't put the toothpick in her mouth.

Dinner should be a family project. . . not just mom's chore alone.

✔ **Sketch out meals for the coming week.** Instead of scrambling as dinner time approaches, take a few minutes on Sundays to decide what you'll serve for dinner each night of the week—or at the very least the next night. Unless you're planning to go shopping every day, you need to know what you'll be cooking each day so you can make sure you have all the ingredients.

✔ **Take advantage of down times for food prep.** Any food prep you can do in advance will help make dinner go more smoothly. If you have a late sleeper or a napper, do the prep work when your child is in bed. Even if it's 10 p.m. when everyone's in bed, you can store things in the fridge for the next day—a great way to get ahead and feel ready and accomplished.

✔ **Keep your pantry well-stocked.** Staples such as pasta, pasta sauce, canned beans, rice, soups, flour, sugar, herbs, olive oil, and other ingredients can go into your favorite recipes.

✔ **Share the load.** Give each child an assignment that he or she can own, such as setting the table or unloading the dishwasher's silverware basket. It's not only a great way to take the load off Mom's shoulders; it's also a good opportunity for teaching children how to cook. Dinner time should be a family project, and kids of all ages should be involved—Dad too! It may not always be realistic, but it's at least worth trying, if not for at least one night a week.

* **Children 2 to 5:** Kids as young as 2 (and under) can put napkins on the table, stir ingredients, hand you spice containers, be in charge of listening for the oven timer, etc. Older children can take part by mixing, measuring (great math lesson), setting the table, clearing the table, helping with dishes, etc. Taking part will not only increase the quality time your children get to spend with you, but it will give them a sense of ownership in the meal, increasing the chance they'll be happy to eat it and fostering a great sense of self accomplishment when they get to eat what they've made. Children this age can also help pick out recipes from a colorful cookbook, help with a shopping list, and help you hunt for items at the supermarket. You might also want to ask them to prepare a centerpiece, something artistic they can make while you're preparing dinner.

* **Children 6 to 9** can make a salad, wash fruit, and even help you assemble ingredients for a dinner recipe. They can also help set the table, carry dishes, fill the salt and pepper shakers, and so on. Have them be your mini *sous chef* and get them washing lettuce, spinning salad, etc. They might even get a kick out of writing place cards. Sometimes, planning seating arrangements alleviates the "I was sitting there" arguments.

* **Children 10 to 12** can do more advanced cooking with parental supervision. Have them assemble ingredients out of the pantry for you, write a list of what you need to get, and act as executive chefs, overseeing preparation.

* **13 and up:** Teenagers can coordinate the cooking and cleanup and supervise their younger siblings in the kitchen. Kids who get home from school before their parents can pull out the ingredients you need, provided you leave a list. Depending on their ages, you can teach them to prepare some of these items like rinsing the lettuce, chopping the onions, forming the meatballs, etc.

✔ **Eliminate distractions.** Remind everyone (including your husband) what the rules are during family dinner: No TV, letting the answering machine pick up the phone, no cell phones, no texting, no computer usage. It might be a challenge at first, but lessening the distractions lets your kids know that spending time together at mealtime is the most important thing.

Meal-Prep Time-Savers

While getting the family to the table requires some finesse, getting the food to the table relies on organization. Consider the following:

● **Map your menus on the computer.** The computer has made our lives easier in so many ways, why not with this one? Storing everything in one place where you can cut and paste a shopping list makes it easier. You can even have your kids and husband add to this with their favorites. Creating a template with detailed products under specific categories like dairy/meat/produce/seasonings/snacks/drinks/baking/etc., is another way to go. That way you simply print out the same list, put it on the fridge and have everyone circle or highlight what they need. For those *really* organized folks, map out your grocery shopping template according to the aisles in the grocery store. That makes going in and out of a store that much more efficient.

● **Do grocery shopping after the kids are in bed.** You'll whiz through the store with less frustration and it's often less crowded. If you have school-age kids or those in daycare, going early in the morning is another possibility. I'm a summer person, but I have to admit, I love winter because I can go to the grocery store in the morning before work and leave everything in my cold car. Luckily, my office has a large fridge, and I'm not shy if I need to bring in a few items in to store for the day.

● **Keep an insulated bag in your car.** By keeping a cold/hot pack in my car, I can always pick up last-minute items when it is convenient for me and not worry about them sitting in my car.

● **Choose meats or other proteins that can be used for several meals during a week.** Make meatloaf the same week that you make tacos, and make roast chicken the same week you make soup and sandwiches. Think in terms of combinations. If you have salad fixings and leftover taco meat, make taco salads, and make hamburgers from leftover meatloaf.

● **Do double duty.** Making two batches of stew or lasagna doesn't require much more time than making one. Double your recipe, and freeze the extra food for a quick meal another night.

● **Embrace leftovers.** Often, a simple pasta made the day or two

Continued on next page

Meal-Prep Time-Savers (continued)

before can be revived with a few chopped tomatoes, some garlic, and olive oil. Leftover chicken can be cut up and put over rice or thrown into pasta.

- **Think prepackaged.** Cut prep time by using prepackaged items like bag salads, jar sauces, refrigerated rolls, and canned or frozen fruits and vegetables.

- **Multi-task.** Cut up lots of veggies at once. Store them in the fridge until you need them. It's easy to whip up a healthy stir-fry or put out a plate of carrots and some hummus for healthy snacking (including for yourself).

- **Stock up on non-perishables.**

Avoid last-minute trips to the grocery store by keeping often-used items such as rice, pasta, and frozen vegetables on hand.

- **Love your freezer.** When you go to the grocery store, buy more chicken and meat and, heck, even frozen pizza, the busy mom's staple (along with chicken nuggets). That way, there's always something in the freezer to defrost for dinner. If you can, keep a second freezer in your garage or basement so you can store even more. It's always great to have a stockpile for unplanned moments, especially if you have hungry teens and their hungry friends.

✔ **Slow down.** Children tend to eat more slowly than adults, so plan on enough time for kids to finish their meals. An unhurried timetable creates a better environment for digestion too. Don't eat and run. Dinnertime might only be half an hour when you start, but try to aim for an hour because this gives you enough time to relax, start a conversation, and enjoy a meal together. Instead of rushing through your dinner, take a few extra minutes to relax before cleaning up. While it would be ideal if dinner could be an hour of uninterrupted family time, it's not always possible. Better to have a half hour of no TV, no phone calls, no computer, than an hour of dinner with tons of distractions.

✔ **Cook up table topics.** Remember, bringing your family together is not about serving a gourmet meal, but rather about interacting and reconnecting. You may be tempted to talk to your husband about something that happened at work, but don't leave the children out of the loop. Share your job anecdotes in terms they can understand. Ask about their day, talk about the family's plans for the weekend, get their ideas for family projects. Think of age-appropriate discussions, perhaps something interesting you saw in the news that week, or some news you heard about in your community. It's also fun to ask your kids out-there questions, like:

Meal-Prep Time-Savers (continued)

- **Plan something easy.** Offer "breakfast night," when you serve easy-to-make a.m. favorites, or soup-and-sandwich night, or even just a "hodgepodge/we love leftovers" night, and get your kids to think of creative ideas for what's left over from the day before. Maybe even offer a prize (an extra scoop of ice cream?) for the child who comes up with the most inventive dish.

- **Beef up your spice rack.** The key to ensuring dinner does not become boring is not in the basic ingredients but in the spices. Try meatloaf with a liberal amount of tarragon; same basic meal with a unique flavor.

Next time, add curry powder, and so on.

- **Consider starting a monthly meal exchange program with other moms in the same boat.** I know. I know. We're all busy. Who has time? But this was sug-

Continued on next page

"If you could be any animal, what would it be and why?" or "What movie star would play you in a movie, and why?" or "What would you do if you were a millionaire?" Many parents have a game called Highs and Lows, in which each person talks about the best and worst part of their day. One dad I know starts out by asking what the rumor of the day was at middle school. Another mom starts off the conversation asking, "What was the one thing you'd change about today?"

It's also a nice idea to take turns saying something meaningful before eating—allowing everyone to give input, not just a parent. Simple things like thanking the person who did the cooking, or talking about those less fortunate can give perspective.

✔ **Keep the conversation inclusive.** Don't let one person take over. On the other hand, be respectful of the fact that your kids, depending on their age (I'm thinking tweens and teens here) may not want to talk at all. Respect that. Give them time to get used to this new "we're talking at the table" thing. Allow them to stew (no pun intended), or be moody, and just plain be angry that their dinner routine has been altered. But do eventually let them know they will have to join in the conversation. Use "I" statements like "I know you're upset I've changed

Meal-Prep Time-Savers (continued)

gested to me by a couple of moms and, though it might sound like a pie-in-the-sky-shoot-for-the-stars kind of strategy, depending on where you live and who you know, it could be worth it. . . especially when you add wine and girl talk. It doesn't have to be a lot of work if good conversations (and Chardonnay) become part of the equation.

Here's the deal: Once a month, cook enough for two dinners. Stash one in the freezer, and take the other to meet up with the group for swapping. Then go home with four other meals, and put them in the freezer alongside the extra one you made for your family. Suddenly you're stocked up with a variety of easy, home-made meals, and all it took was a night with your girlfriends. Not a bad excuse for a girl's night, eh?

- **Do all your cooking on Sunday.** Prepare meals for Monday and Tuesday so your week starts off less stressful.

- **Consider a crock pot.** Many moms swear by these slow cookers, into which you toss food in the morning, and by evening you have a delicious meal.

- **Same goes for a stir fry.** If you have the right ingredients, i.e., the right cooking utensils, cooking is a lot easier—and faster.

- **Get a countertop grill.** Another easy way to cook/grill indoors and

the dinner hour on you, but this is our new family rule, and we're going to discuss something at the table. Unless you want me to bring a new topic to the table every night, it would be nice if you thought of something." Or say "I know you're not happy with this new arrangement and understand it might take you some time. I'll give you two weeks to get used to it, but eventually you're going to have to contribute."

✔ **No nagging.** Avoid topics like: "You never clean your room/feed the dog/take out the trash." No nagging also means parents should not push food. Encourage your kids to try things, but don't insist on a clean plate. You want a healthy discussion, not one that can fuel eating issues. These topics can be brought up outside the dinner time conversation. You do not want dinner time to be a battleground.

✔ **Manners matter.** This is your chance to teach life-long skills. This includes being respectful, with no teasing allowed at the table, and making sure everyone stays at the table until the last person finishes eating. While each family member

Meal-Prep Time-Savers (continued)

prepare a healthy dinner fast.

● **Think about joining a local CSA.** CSA stands for Community Supported Agriculture. You'll get a box or bag of organic, locally-grown produce delivered once a week to a neighborhood spot near you. You'll not only feel good about the produce you're feeding your kids, but it saves shopping time and supports a local farmer (I'm a big believer in supporting local businesses.) It's also a great way to meet like-minded shoppers and find new ways to get your kids eating fresh food. Go to LocalHarvest. org for information about finding a CSA near you.

speaks, everyone else should try their best to listen and not interrupt. It's also nice to tell your kids how much you appreciate them working towards this new dinner plan to sit down together.

✔ **Invite company.** Let your children bring a friend or two or invite a neighbor. This teaches your kids about how being hospitable and taking care of others and sets your home up as a social hub. It also teaches your kids how to entertain others. And you'll learn more about your children when you see them interact with their friends.

✔ **Set the stage for togetherness.** Clear any clutter off the table, put fresh flowers on the table, add a tablecloth, light candles, make it special. Go a step further and make a point of serving dinner at the dining room table a couple of times a week.

✔ **Introduce new foods.** Providing a different food taste at dinner tends to liven up any discussion, as well as expand the family horizons.

Did you know?

Teenagers who regularly eat dinner with their families have healthier body images, higher grades and are less likely to use drugs or alcohol.

SOURCE: THE UNIVERSITY OF MINNESOTA AND THE NATIONAL CENTER ON ADDICTION AND SUBSTANCE ABUSE AT COLUMBIA UNIVERSITY

✔ **Be creative.** Spice up dinner with picnics on the living room floor, TV trays on the porch, or simply by setting up a buffet in the dining room. Think like your child's elementary school teacher. Remember crazy Fridays or upside-down Tuesdays? You can do the same with dinner to make it something your family looks forward to, simply by giving it a theme. One of my tried and true methods: Decorating for the seasons—for the opposite time frame, e.g., giving the kitchen table a beach theme in winter (with easy summer foods like hot dogs and hamburgers, potato salad, and corn), a scattering of shells and sea glass on the kitchen table and, sometimes, paper plates in red, white, and blue, or beach scenes. Same for winter in summer: Talking about our favorite cold activities, and serving chili or a hearty pot roast, and maybe hot chocolate with cookies for dessert.

An ethnic food night is another way to add some creativity and variety and get your kids involved. One night everything you serve might be German, and another night it might be Italian, or Chinese, or Hawaiian. Sometimes, just piling chicken or beef with a new spice on top of rice is all you need to do to make it different. For Hawaiian night, I usually just add pineapple to everything. It doesn't have to be fancy—and definitely does not have to be something that takes a lot of effort. It's just something that takes some forethought. Dinner is *always* at the back of my mind: How to make it more fun, more enjoyable, something my family looks forward to, and is proud to bring their friends to our house for. Which is why when I go to our local crafts store, I often stock up on theme decorations and store them in my basement for times like these. Usually I go *after* the holiday, i.e., Thanksgiving, Christmas, Valentine's Day, so everything—from paper plates to napkins to lei necklaces—is on sale, making this a small investment.

Kids should help with clean up at a young age.

Of course you can also be creative without the fancy extras. For years, taco night was the big hit in our house, and often the simplest. Just a row of help-yourself bowls filled with cooked beef, refried beans, cheese, lettuce, salsa, and taco shells. Start a fondue night or create-your-own-pizza evening or even a let's-raid-the-pantry possibility, using an array of leftovers and staples. Or make it a family-style night, and tell kids they can eat whatever they want as long as they eat two or three spoonfuls of something (and at least one thing must be green). All are easy ways to get out of your dinner routine (some might say rut) and slow down mealtime, allowing for more time to talk.

✔ **Clean up together.** This should be a ritual as well, where someone loads the dishwasher, clears the table, puts the mustard back in the fridge. Mom or Dad shouldn't be saddled with all the work. Prep and cleanup are all part of mealtime, and kids should be involved at an age-appropriate level.

✔ **Don't worry if you don't have time to cook.** Your favorite take-out can work just as well as a home-cooked meal for gathering the family. The most important thing is to eat and talk together. I'm a big fan of prepared foods.

Mom Tip

"The 10 must-haves in my kitchen:

1. Whole grain products (pasta, bread, brown rice)—completely versatile, and an easy way to get fiber into kids.

2. Frozen fruits and veggies—this way I can sneak antioxidants into each meal without having to have fresh on hand.

3. Cast iron skillet—the best way to cook meat, it's a cheap, durable cooking tool that adds iron to everything cooked in it.

4. Lowfat dairy products—yogurt, milk and cottage cheese. These go into recipes so I can ensure my family gets enough calcium.

5. Dried beans—an excellent low-fat, high-fiber source of protein. I cook this every week in my slow-cooker to make soups, dips and burritos.

6. Sea salt—tastes saltier than iodized salts, so I can use less (and reduce the sodium level in my cooking).

7. Good knives—make chopping a pleasure, meaning I'm likelier to cook at home.

8. Windowbox garden—I have a planter of basil, rosemary and thyme, with other herbs being added seasonally. This way, I can add flavor and nutrients to dishes without spending a fortune.

9. Deli containers that have been washed—instead of spending a ton on Tupperware, I use deli containers for leftovers.

10. Individually frozen salmon filets—so I can scale up (or down) recipes easily and ensure that my family is getting Omega 3s."

—Jill Houk, Chicago, IL, mom of one, age 10, CenteredChef.com

✔ **Breathe.** Take a deep breath. Life isn't perfect. The milk will spill. The kids will fight. The meat may be slightly overcooked, the potatoes a tad mushy. But you're trying. The fact that your kids see that is more important than you know.

Nipping TV in the Bud

Let's address the big fat gorilla in the room right away. TV has become our electronic babysitter. When we desperately need some time to ourselves, even to chop vegetables or return a phone call, it gives us ten minutes. It's large screen and colorful, pixilated images are there when we want to get dinner on the table without someone clinging to our legs. And it's there when we're just plain exhausted from a long day out and need to get our children to sit for (heaven forbid) two seconds while we decompress. I'm not against TV. In fact I've used it as a means of distraction more times than I want to admit. (My daughter Corey's first word was Elmo, so that should tell you something.) But it doesn't belong at the dinner table.

You only need to read the statistics to "get" why:

✱ The average household has the TV on in the background for more than seven hours per day. Children watch almost three hours of TV each day.

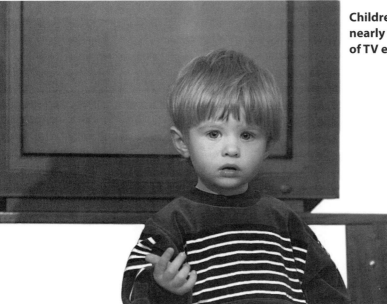

Children watch nearly three hours of TV each day.

* People viewing more than three hours of TV per day are twice as likely to be obese as those watching less than one hour per day.

* As TV viewing time increases, so does snacking, while physical activity decreases.

* Children increase their risk of becoming obese by seven percent for every hour of TV watched on weekends at the age of five.

* Children watching more than two hours per day on weekends are more likely to become obese adults.

And it continues with other jaw-dropping facts:

* The average American youth spends 900 hours in school. . . and 1,500 hours per year watching TV.

* The average child will watch 8,000 murders on TV before finishing elementary school. By age 18, the average American has seen 200,000 acts of violence on TV, including 40,000 murders.

* Several studies have shown that heavy television viewing by children contributes to the development of attention-deficit and other behavioral disorders.

If those weren't scary enough, how about:

* Fifty-four percent of four- to six-year-olds, when asked to choose between watching TV and spending time with their fathers, preferred television.

* American parents on average spend less than 40 minutes each week in meaningful conversations with their children.

* Sixty-six percent of Americans watch television while eating dinner.

TV is a powerful toxin. Press the remote, and we're all soon glued. We put food in our mouths and don't even taste it. We forget to speak to each other. We even lose track of how much food we just shoveled into our mouths. Is it so much to ask for an hour that we turn it off?

Family dinner time should mean time spent together. Bottom line: If you never introduce the TV at mealtime, your kids won't miss it. Including *not* putting it on when they are babies and you are sitting with your husband. Believe me: They absorb it.

And so: No TV at the dinner table. *Period.* It should be your hard-fast rule. But if you're like most American moms (including me), you've already allowed it... which means now you have to take it away.

Have a family meeting to discuss your new house rules.

How To Take TV Away Without a Revolt

The fact that you can tape shows or watch them on your computer is a good enough reason to explain to your kids that you're not taking away the TV forever: Just for dinnertime. Any change in routine, however, especially a big one like taking away the boob tube, requires a group discussion.

Make sure, first, that your significant other is on the same page with you and ready to present a united front. Then bring the topic to your children. Obviously, if they are babies or toddlers, this might not be necessary, but if your kids are school-age or older and already used to one routine, you need to brief them on your new rules. Use "I" sentences, e.g., "I've always wanted to have us sit and talk around the dinner table the way I used to as a kid and, though we haven't done that a lot recently, it's something I feel strongly about that we should do." Or: "I've always dreamed of sitting around the dinner table and talking," or "I've been frustrated with the way our family handles dinner together and, so, I've thought of a way to change it."

✔ **Give your kids some sense of control.** Use those "I" sentences to let your kids know you understand their frustration at rearranging schedules to fit in this new routine, e.g., "Ideally, I'd like to start this new rule tomorrow night, but since I know that may be hard for you, we can start next Monday, or what do you think is realistic?" Or "I'd like to start at 6 p.m. every night,

Mom Tip

"To get my kids talking at the dinner table, we play the 'adjective game', where each person comes up with an adjective and asks, 'What's the _____est thing that happened to you today?' This frequently results in really weird conversations, about the 'smelliest 'thing, the 'creepiest', etc., but it does get a conversation going."
—Lauren Mayer, San Mateo, CA, mom of two, 13 and 16

"We always start dinner with grace; in addition to giving thanks for our food, it signals the beginning of dinner to my kids."
—Laura Dihel, Bartlett, IL, mom of two, ages 3 years and 16 months

"One of the few family 'rituals' we have is holding hands around the table and each person says thank you for something they're grateful for that day. Our thank yous, or lack of ideas for a thank you, as well as our tones of voice, etc. give cues for conversation. Family meals are the heart of our closeness."
—Ruth Greenwood, Princeton, NJ, mom of two, ages 12 and 1

but if you have a TV show you really love, and it doesn't end until later, we could do 6:30 p.m." Don't sway from your ultimate goal: Dinner as a family. But *do* let them know they have a say in the matter. It will help them be more on board.

✔ **Start slow.** If you watched TV five nights a week when dinner was served, change it to four nights. Announce to your family your new intentions and how important it is to you to have an hour with no interruptions—just family time. Everyone can pick their favorite shows and record them for later. If they argue, complain, and say they don't watch a lot of TV in the first place, have them prove it to you. Keep a TV journal so they can see how they are spending their time. Remind them, too, that you are not taking their shows away—they can tape them for later. Be firm. You are their parent, not their BFF. If they give you a hard time, remind them that *you* can turn off the TV, or *they* can.

✔ **Don't make a big deal.** Don't all of a sudden start breaking out the good china and candles and dusting off your *Joy of Cooking* just for your first TV-free meal. It should not be *special.* . . just your regularly scheduled dinner hour. Remember to keep the conversation light. Ask them about their favorite TV shows or their favorite TV characters. Talk about ones that you grew up with and how they are different.

✔ **Turn on the music.** Background music, just like in a restaurant, can be soothing. Choose some jazz or classical. And involve your kids by letting them be in charge of the music one or two nights a week.

3

An Organized Pantry is the Best Stress-Reliever I Know

If you're anything like me, your food **pantry is like your clothes closet.** Just like I have ten white shirts and maybe one red and one navy, I also have about five boxes of the same cereal, little to no sugar, and virtually no jelly. My husband likes to make fun of how I'm constantly buying the same things over and over, yet keep forgetting some of the staples we really need, like vegetable oil, Worcestershire sauce, and sugar. More often than not, he also grumbles about the waste of money, as he sees no reason why we have three ketchups, four boxes of crackers, and two huge jars of mayo, one of which almost always expires before I find it.

As much as I hate to admit it, he's right. Most times my fridge/freezer/pantry/pick a cabinet/any cabinet has been so jammed with junk that I have no idea what's where, or even

My 12 Pantry Must-Haves

1. Bread crumbs
2. Olive oil
3. Soy or barbeque sauce
4. Salt, pepper, garlic
5. Balsamic vinegar
6. Pasta and/or rice
7. Tomato sauce or forms of tomatoes in cans
8. Some fresh, frozen or canned veggies—a bag of spinach, frozen string beans, canned corn—things you can cut up and put in an omelet or make into a veggie side dish
9. Peanut butter
10. Flour
11. Eggs
12. Wine (for the cook!)

if I have something in the first place. With so much hunger in the world, I'm embarrassed to admit that I've thrown out a lot of food that, had I been more organized, would not have gone to waste (hello freezer burn and those unrecognizable blobs wrapped in foil).

This disorganization not only annoyed my husband (and frankly, is not the best lesson to pass on to my girls), but also frustrated me because I was doing exactly the opposite of what I wanted to do. Who knew there were five boxes of the same kind of cereal way in the back of the pantry? When I looked in, I saw zero. So when I went to the food store, what do you think was top of mind for me to buy? MORE CEREAL!

It sounds obvious, but the trick to getting dinner on the table is having the right foods in the house to begin with. Stuff that you know you have. And that you'll use. And that is organized and carefully placed where you can find it. Which is why, if you want to strategize and streamline your dinner planning, you need a well-stocked pantry filled with basic staples. And that includes the contents of your freezer and fridge.

This is the "STOP. Do not pass GO" part of this book. Consider it your attitude adjuster. Yes, it will take time. Yes, it's a pain. But I promise it will help your life immensely. As much as you might hate to hear it, you need a well-stocked pantry in some semblance of order (think like items with like items; i.e., cereal with cereal, condiments with condiments, pasta with pasta), as well as the occasional see-through container, ideally with some kind of label, for mealtimes to get easier.

Pantry Basics

Remember, this is just a guide. Each family is different and may need more of some, less of another.

BASICS

- ❏ Applesauce
- ❏ Baking powder
- ❏ Baking soda
- ❏ Baking or pancake mix
- ❏ Bread
- ❏ Bread crumbs
- ❏ Broths: vegetable, chicken, beef, or bouillon cubes
- ❏ Cereal
- ❏ Chocolate chips
- ❏ Cocoa
- ❏ Coffee
- ❏ Condiments: ketchup, mustard, mayonnaise
- ❏ Cooking spray
- ❏ Cornstarch
- ❏ Dip mixes
- ❏ Drinks: juice, bottled water, sports drinks
- ❏ Evaporated and condensed milk
- ❏ Flour, all-purpose
- ❏ Food storage items: baggies, airtight containers, aluminum foil
- ❏ Honey
- ❏ Jelly
- ❏ Mac and cheese

- ❏ Maple syrup
- ❏ Marinades
- ❏ Oatmeal
- ❏ Oils: olive, safflower, sunflower, or grapeseed
- ❏ Pasta
- ❏ Paper goods: paper towels, napkins
- ❏ Peanut butter
- ❏ Rice
- ❏ Salad dressings
- ❏ Sauces: soy or tamari, tabasco, teriyaki, Worcestershire, barbeque
- ❏ Sugar: granulated white, powdered, and brown

- ❏ Tea
- ❏ Tortilla wraps
- ❏ Vanilla
- ❏ Vinegar: white, cider, balsamic

SNACKS

- ❏ Chips (potato and tortilla)
- ❏ Cookie and brownie mixes
- ❏ Cookies
- ❏ Crackers
- ❏ Granola Bars
- ❏ Popcorn
- ❏ Raisins
- ❏ Trail Mix

Pantry Basics

HERBS & SPICES

- ❏ Basil
- ❏ Bay leaves
- ❏ Cayenne pepper
- ❏ Chili powder
- ❏ Cinnamon
- ❏ Crushed red pepper
- ❏ Cumin
- ❏ Dill
- ❏ Garlic powder
- ❏ Garlic salt
- ❏ Ground ginger
- ❏ Italian seasoning
- ❏ Nutmeg
- ❏ Onion powder
- ❏ Oregano
- ❏ Paprika
- ❏ Parsley
- ❏ Pepper
- ❏ Rosemary
- ❏ Sage
- ❏ Salt
- ❏ Seafood seasonings
- ❏ Tarragon
- ❏ Thyme

IN THE FRIDGE

- ❏ Cheese
- ❏ Cream cheese
- ❏ Bacon
- ❏ Butter or margarine
- ❏ Eggs
- ❏ Garlic
- ❏ Ginger
- ❏ Grated parmesan
- ❏ Lemon juice
- ❏ Milk
- ❏ Salsa
- ❏ Sour cream

IN THE FREEZER

- ❏ Bread/bagels/rolls
- ❏ Butter
- ❏ French fries
- ❏ Frozen berries
- ❏ Frozen breakfast pancakes or waffles
- ❏ Frozen veggies
- ❏ Garlic bread
- ❏ Hamburger meat
- ❏ Hot dogs
- ❏ Ice cream
- ❏ Meat sauce
- ❏ Pizza dough
- ❏ Store-bought appetizers
- ❏ Store-bought frozen pizza

PRODUCE

- ❏ Carrots
- ❏ Celery
- ❏ Cucumbers
- ❏ Fresh herbs
- ❏ Fruit: grapes, apples, berries, depending on the season
- ❏ Garlic, whole
- ❏ Lemons
- ❏ Onions
- ❏ Pre-washed lettuce and greens by the bag
- ❏ Potatoes
- ❏ Tomatoes

CANNED GOODS

- ❏ Beans: kidney, black beans, refried
- ❏ Chili
- ❏ Olives: canned, pitted and non-pitted, Nicoise, calamata, olive paste
- ❏ Soups
- ❏ Tomatoes: diced, crushed
- ❏ Tomato paste
- ❏ Tuna and other fish
- ❏ Vegetables: corn, peas, string beans

It sounds simple, but the trick to getting dinner on the table is having food in your pantry.

Reasons To Be Happy With Your Pantry

How do I know this will be worth it and help take the chaos out of the dinner hour?

✔ **Reason to be happy #1:** Well-stocked pantries are protection against unexpected events. They're like your bomb shelter so that the household never runs out of commonly used products. You'll never have to rant to your husband, asking why you've suddenly run out of coffee when you swear you bought coffee last week. Ideally, the essential pantry items will keep for a long time in storage, and fresh, perishable foods will be regularly used before they spoil.

✔ **Reason to be happy #2:** A well-stocked pantry saves time, money, and stress, both in the kitchen and in your relationships. (This helps manage who used what last and who didn't replace it/write it down.) You'll cut down the number of trips to the grocery store—a plus when you have small kids in tow—and you'll actually have more time to get dinner on the table. Plus, when you or your husband do have to run to the store, you'll find it a more streamlined and efficient process. There's no excuse any more (or at least less excuses): When you have basic pantry items in the house, you'll only need to buy perishables and depleted pantry items.

Include your fridge and freezer as part of your pantry.

Mom Tip

"I splurged on a vacuum sealer a number of years ago and have not regretted it. It makes frozen soups and leftovers boil-in-bag-able for future use. I'm also big into freezing individual chicken pieces, then placing them in storage bags for use in crock pot recipes. You can pull out just the pieces you need, and they'll fit in the crock pot since they're not in one large frozen block."

—Michelle Levine, Houston, TX, mom of two, ages 9 and 13

✔ **Reason to be happy #3:** Your grocery costs will go down as you stock your pantry with frugal finds (think store brands, also known as private-label) and good deals (using promotions and coupons at the grocery store for stuff you need, not impulse buys). This avoids the unneeded waste of expired yogurt, stale cereal, mayo, and other items.

Remember: Your refrigerator and freezer are part of the pantry, as are your cupboards, shelves, or floor space in a closet. Heck, I even count the steps going down to the basement where I store my trash bags and paper towels as part of my pantry. Fair warning: This will take time. (A rainy Sunday is perfect.) But it's worth it. This call to action isn't so much a plan as it is a lifestyle adjustment. It will save you time. Most of it will save your sanity.

Part of that sanity means that if your time is really constrained, think small bites. In other words, do what you can reasonably handle (the overriding theme of this book). You don't have to buy everything at once. Just purchase what you eat fairly often, and in small quantities so foods stay fresh. Build up your pantry gradually.

Or simply bite the bullet (and the large bill) and go pantry shopping. You can even make it an activity/game with the kids, checking off everything on your list as you go up and down the aisles, and making the event like a scavenger hunt. If you're really strapped for time, simply let your fingers do the walking. . . on your keyboard, and order from Peapod, Fresh Direct, or food delivery service, providing they deliver in your area.

Customize It

One more word about the pantry: It's yours, so cater it to your family's needs and taste-buds, and don't stock up on items you won't use. Each family's pantry will vary according to their own preferences and standard of living. For instance, those with young children will most likely fill their pantries with lots of cereal, formula, and child-friendly snack foods. Non-cooks may be heavy on microwave entrées, soups, and frozen pizzas. Those with growing teens may be into buying bulk sports drinks, to-go snacks, tons of pasta, and extra protein. It's your list, your life. The following words of wisdom are meant as a general guideline.

Mom Tip

"Stick to a master list, always buying the same staples each week. Keep a 'wish-list' of items you'd like to try or splurge on once a week. For example, buy your usual dairy, fruits, veggies, and meats, but pick up a new spice or new fresh herb. Maybe try panko crumbs instead of regular bread crumbs, or avocado oil instead of olive oil as a way to stay on budget but mix up your routine."
—Dawn Viola, Orlando, FL, mom of one, age 9

Top Time-Savers:

* Precooked chicken breast tenders, slices, or cuts

* Frozen or canned vegetables and fruit

* Bottled marinades

* A garlic pepper dry rub

Place like items close to one another so it's easier to find things when you need them.

> ## Mom Tip
>
> *"In my fridge, there is always yogurt, milk, assorted cheeses, maple syrup, Asian sauces, Dijon mustard, and mayonnaise. Vegetables including carrots, celery, cabbage, and other root vegetables. Then spices and herbs: Dry thyme, dry mint, cumin, chili powder, cinnamon, nutmeg, salt, and pepper. I can't live without pasta, rice, flour, natural sugar, honey, nuts, seeds, and a bin of potatoes and onions."*
>
> —Laurie Zerga, Alameda, CA, founder of Chef-K®, culinary health education for kids, mom of two, ages 19 and 21

Act like your mother (or mother-in-law). In other words, be ruthless. Go through your kitchen like you would your kid's overstuffed dresser. Take everything out. Assess it. Some things are not necessary; some things are. What you no longer need (meaning you haven't used it in a year), give to a food pantry (if it's still edible). Or toss it. Be honest with yourself. If you can't remember why the heck you ever bought it (a recipe you swore you'd try with an exotic ingredient you'd previously never heard of), get rid of it. Get your kids to help. They can be in charge of the "what stays" and "what goes" piles.

Keep like items together. . .

After you've put everything out on the table and given it a good once-over, start stocking. Place like items together so that they are easier to locate, retrieve, and replace. For example, put canned veggies and beans together, pasta and rice, candy and cookies, chips and crackers, sauces and condiments.

...And in order...

Arrange and rotate items so that the oldest ones are at the front and in line to be used first. Using and replacing food on a regular basis ensures that nothing gets so old that it loses its palatability or nutritional value, and that cans and jars don't sit around long enough to rust through. Again, kids can help in restacking items.

...And where you can see them.

The middle shelves, the ones that are easiest to access, should be used for commonly used items. Arrange boxed goods so you can read what is inside without having to remove the package. Heavy items, such as large quantities of bottled water, can be placed on the floor of the pantry while lighter, bulky, non-food items, like paper towels, can be placed on the upper shelves. For safety purposes, store all cleaning products away from food and out of the reach of children.

Keep small amounts of the items you use everyday such as tea, coffee, sugar, salt, etc., in reachable, sensible places in your kitchen, e.g., the coffee by the coffee maker, the salt by the stove, etc. Store larger, back-up quantities of these ingredients in your pantry. Make sure that where you place things makes sense to your life.

The goal here is making it convenient and logical to get from the pantry to the counter, so you're spending less time rummaging for ingredients and more time actually sitting at the din-

Mom Tips

"*Do all your shopping in one place. We use our favorite pantry items and frozen staples and limit the ingredients to as few as possible without sacrificing taste or quality. Use time-saving prepared ingredients, such as prepared sauces, marinated meats, washed/pre-cut vegetables, bagged salads, and other lifesavers, such as frozen pre-cooked brown rice. "*

—Deana Gunn, San Diego, CA, mom of two, ages 5 and 6, and Wona Miniati, San Francisco, CA, mom of two, ages 3 and 5, authors of *Cooking with Trader Joe's*, CookingWithTraderJoes.com

"*A few years ago, I created a meal spreadsheet in Excel, and this has helped me to plan my meals. This meal plan is also helpful because you can take a look at what is in your freezer and remember to pull it out the night before. Also, it helps with the 'What's for dinner mom whine,' as the kids can see that if they don't like tonight's dinner, maybe they'll like tomorrow's.*"

—Betty Huotari, Fenton, MI, mom of two, ages 10 and 11

Write down what you need and what you're running low on.

ner table with your family. The sense of order also helps your kids as they get older (as well as any other members of your household), as they will know where everything goes and can help to retrieve and replace items.

Pen it in.

Yes, it sounds a bit neurotic, but if you start now, it will become a habit. . . and a good habit to boot. Date everything so you and your family can always be confident that what you're eating is safe. Just grab a Sharpie® and note the month/year on the canned goods and boxed goods as you unpack them. This is another fun activity for school-age children who enjoy being mother's helpers.

Use your librarian skills.

Keep a running inventory of what you have ten of (in my case mayo) and what you need more of. It's a great idea to keep a blackboard, dry-erase board, or pad and paper handy so once someone finishes the Cheerios®, for example, that person can put it on the list. Make a shopping list as you work. Whenever you're running low on peanut butter or pasta, make sure that's the first thing on your shopping list the next time you head to the grocery store.

Think storage solutions.

Once you've gone through everything, it's easier to see what your needs are. You might need plastic containers, a soup/can rack, or a pantry door organizer. Depending on the product, plastic containers are often less bulky than product packaging and take up less space. Also, if you open cereal, it will go stale faster in the box.

Buy in bulk when it makes sense.

Don't be seduced by a great price. Buying large quantities of an item is only worth it if you use it a lot, and if you have room to store it. Bulk shopping buys can be good investments. By purchasing items that you use frequently from wholesalers and warehouse stores, you'll save money on non-food pantry items such as paper products and on items that have at least a one-year shelf-life. Remember to put in air-tight containers what could feasibly go bad.

Stock up on ingredients for your tried and true meals.

Make sure you have the ingredients in multiples for the recipes you prepare the most; that way you'll always have what you need on hand to make it a few times. So, if a regular recipe calls for a can of diced tomatoes, buy three or four.

Note the cost savings.

With a shopping list full of items you need, as opposed to grab-and-go last-minute purchases, you buy only what's necessary. Plus, your now-organized pantry gives you a better idea of the non-perishable items and other products with a long shelf-life so that when they are on sale, you can buy them knowing they won't go to waste.

Mom Tips

"Cook dried beans in bulk and freeze in smaller containers: Better tasting and cheaper than canned beans. Also, whenever I roast or bake a chicken, bones go into the freezer until I need stock. Then, when I make the stock, leftover stock gets massively reduced (to save room) and placed in the freezer. "

—Laura Tabacca, Oxford, OH, mom of two, ages 3 and 4

"I spend one day a month freezing a bunch of meals. It takes a lot of time on the one day, but you free up most of your evenings during the month, making life so much easier. Can't think of doing a month's worth in one day? Do a week's worth or two weeks worth."

—Tricia Callahan, Dayton, OH, mom of two under age 2

"When I get extra chicken breasts on sales, I cook them all, then shred, cube and slice them. I keep it portioned in the freezer for soups, chicken salad, quick sandwich wraps, salads, or any kind of casserole-type items."

—Michelle Levine, Houston, TX, mom of two, ages 9 and 13

Love Your Freezer

I've always been a freezer fanatic. To me, it just makes sense. You know the food's there, and you know you can defrost it and heat it up. It's how I was brought up. My mom was always big on freezing our meals, making more than enough so there would be extras for a night when she didn't have time to cook. She'd place chicken parmigiana, for example, in tin foil with a handwritten note on top, marking the date she prepared it and what it was. She'd then put it in a zip-lock bag so that on nights she worked late, my sister and I could take out what we wanted and start heating up dinner. Sometimes we all had different things for dinner, but we all ate together.

Another plus: We always had more than enough food. In fact, my mom became a favorite among my high school friends, as they knew, even at the last minute, they were welcome for dinner. Her mantra: The more the merrier. Not to mention, thanks to her school-teacher background, she knew that kids open up and talk more with their friends at the table. And because my friends were so comfortable talking to her, she got a lot of information!

While I haven't been privy to the same gossip (as a writer, my girls know they eventually end up in my stories and hate that), I do follow the same freezer rules. It helps that many items freeze well, such as meats, chicken, fish, vegetables, casserole

Make sure to use the proper storage bags when freezing items.

Some Other Freezing Tips

- Always freeze food as quickly as possible to maintain quality and freshness, and freeze items at 0°F or lower for best quality.

- If you're cooking specifically to freeze something, slightly undercook it, as it will finish cooking once reheated.

- Cool hot foods before you freeze them. Freezing food when hot will only increase the temperature of the freezer and could cause other foods to start defrosting.

- Never re-freeze anything that's been frozen. Even if the food was frozen raw and then cooked, to be extra safe it still shouldn't be re-frozen. If in doubt, throw it out.

- Whatever you do, don't forget to label. This is key.

- Remember the pantry rule: First in, first out.

- Defrost frozen ground meat in the fridge first. Ideally, take it out the night before you plan to serve it. As a general rule, placing food on the counter for a few hours to defrost at room temperature is OK.

dishes, chili, stews, soup, bread, pastries, and cookies.

The secret to freezer-happy dinners is to label your foods. It all goes back to what we discussed earlier about treating your freezer like you do your pantry. And that includes marking and dating items clearly with a Sharpie® or a label and placing the newest food in the bottom or near the back of the freezer, then rotating the older ones forward so they are next in line for use. And though it may sound a bit fanatical, it's also a good idea to post a list of all your frozen food (with dates) near the freezer and check off what is used. To retain the best texture and flavor, most home-frozen foods should be used within six to nine months.

Rules for Freezing Food

To those who swear they hate freezing meals because of freezer burn (basically when air meets frozen food), I say chill out! Once you realize the ease and convenience, you'll soon become a convert. Having pre-frozen food available gives you peace of mind, saves trips to the grocery store, and solves that age-old problem of catering to picky eaters who often don't want the same thing you're having.

Don't Freeze

* High-water-content vegetables (lettuce, to- matoes, celery, etc.)

• Eggs

• Creamed cottage cheese

• Sour cream

• Potatoes

• Cooked pasta (un- less very firm)

• Most spices and extracts

* Cake or pie with custard filling

* Lunch meats

* Mayonnaise

* Sauces thickened with flour or cornstarch, except when used as a binder for other ingredients.

* Light cream (You can freeze milk but it tends to separate. Just shake it well when you defrost.)

* Raw vegetables, unless they have been blanched first

Some rules of thumb:

Rule #1 **Wrap well.** Freezer burn is dehydration of the food caused by improper packing and, though it's not harmful, it does adversely affect the food's texture and color, causing kids to go "eww." Since the last thing you need when trying to get dinner on the table is a picky eater who refuses a meal, you need to make sure you wrap the food correctly in the first place.

Rule #2 **Use the proper storage items;** i.e., freezer bags or containers, foil, or freezer wrap. You can also use heavy-duty plastic containers or jars, but never glass, as the extreme temperatures may cause it to break. Leave some space at the top of containers, as foods will expand during freezing. Try to prevent air coming into the package or moisture from escaping, as these dry out food and affect quality.

Rule #3 **Package foods in meal-sized portions.** This works wonders for moms with carpools to drive and little time to prepare a decent dinner. It also makes it possible to serve three children three different items. If you have more than one piece in a portion, you may want to place a sheet of freezer paper between them to prevent them from sticking together. I'm a big fan of keeping frozen protein of all kinds (ground beef, chicken, fish) in the freezer at all times. That way, you know you always have some kind of meal on hand.

Rule #4 **Repack grocery store items.** To avoid losing texture and flavor, repackage store-bought items promptly (ideally within two hours of purchase; one hour if the temperature is above 90° F), and place them in freezer wraps or bags to ensure secure wrapping. As always, wash hands in hot, soapy water before and after handling raw meat, as well as all utensils, cutting boards, and counters that may have touched raw foods.

If freezing fresh vegetables, it's best to clean them, blanch for two to four minutes, dry, and cut into bite-size or serving-size portions. Blanching simply means dunking the veggies in boiling water for a few seconds and then immediately into ice water to stop the cooking process. This stops enzyme actions that cause loss of flavor, color, texture, and nutrients. It's worth the few extra minutes to blanch, though buying frozen veggies from the get-go is an easy alternative.

Rule #5 **Learn to "flash freeze" like my fellow freezer-fanatical mom Melanie Levin, does.** Items like berries, bananas, peppers, and onions, are great for this, says the Houston, Texas-based mom of two. Prep the food, cube, dice or slice; then lay out on a

Grocery Li
- ☐ Bagels
- ☐ Bread
- ☐ Cream Chee
- ☐ Orange Jui
- ☐ Milk
- ☐ Spaghet
- ☐ Lunchm
- ☐ Chees
- ☐ Grate

Shopping Tips

- ☐ Never go shopping without a list.
- ☐ Shop by price, not by brand.
- ☐ Get a rain check when a sale item is out of stock.
- ☐ Comparison shop, and don't forget to take advantage of deals at drugstore chains (Walgreen's, CVS, etc.).
- ☐ Take advantage of mail-in rebates.
- ☐ Ask if a store accepts competitors' coupons.

Repack grocery-store items within two hours of purchase to keep freshness.

baking sheet and place in your freezer. When solid, place the items in zip-lock baggies, and they're ready to use at will. And you can take advantage of the sale items for use another week/month. The frozen fruits are perfect for smoothies, yogurt parfaits, muffins. The veggies work for all kinds of main dishes, eggs, or quiches.

Melanie takes this one step further and has a baggie just for breakfast tacos/omelets full of peppers, onions, frozen cubed hash brown potatoes, and any pieces of leftover sausage and/or bacon. When needed, she simply warms a small handful of the mix in a sauté pan before adding the eggs. . . and viola! Instant breakfast tacos or omelets without all the prep. Kids can even use this mix for microwave eggs, all of which are great for those nights when you decide to do breakfast for dinner.

Rule #6 **Marinate items before you put them in the freezer.** When they are in the freezer, the molecules expand, pulling in the flavor.

Shopping: It's All About the List

With your pantry organized, it should follow that your list is organized. No need to buy things not on the list. Begin by planning. Many moms use Sunday as their day to meet with their families (even if "meet" means yelling up the stairs) and talk about

At the same time you're cutting and chopping, you should also be labeling, especially if you're putting items in the freezer for later.

the week's meals. Consult your calendar, and think about what will realistically work for the week. If you've kept a template of standard items in your computer, print it out, pin it on the fridge, and have folks circle what they want/need. Some super-organized moms I know even have their computer lists written out in terms of their grocery store aisles so that they know exactly which shopping aisle to tackle first.

I'm not that methodical, though I do like to keep a running tab of the usual suspects in a computer file. That way, I know the stuff for mustard chicken, my standby meal, is always at the ready (chicken, mustard, eggs, bread crumbs).

✔ **Communicate.** This is your starting point: Communicating and making sure every base is covered. If you ask, and your kids/hubby don't respond and don't put it on the list, they'll have to go without or find a way to pick up what they need on their own. Stress upon family members that there is an easy and convenient place in your kitchen for the grocery list. Encourage them to add to it—especially when their favorite items are low and not empty. This is a great way for toddlers and school-age children to learn about planning and organization. They can even practice writing their letters on your list.

✔ **Plot your week.** Admittedly, we all have weeks from hell in which we have no idea how we're going to get Kid #1 to his game when Kid #2 has ballet at exactly the same time. Or when you know you have a PTA meeting and only can fit in a workout at

Did you know?

An almost empty freezer is more expensive to operate than one that is nearly full. Frozen foods help keep their neighbors frozen, so keep your freezer well stocked.

Mom Tip

"When ground beef goes on sale, I buy 20-30 pounds and spend one afternoon cooking it. I stamp it into patties and freeze it between wax sheets. I make taco meat and store it in single-meal-sized freezer bags. I make meatballs, rinse the grease, and then freeze on a cookie sheet and transfer into a bag when frozen. I make spaghetti meat or filling for pastas/pastries. That 30 pounds would feed my family of five 22-25 meals. It takes about three hours to process, but it's worth the time and money savings."

—Julie Parrish, West Linn, OR, mom of three, ages 6, 8, and 9

Top Ten List. . . For Shopping and Cooking Strategically

1 Plan your recipes for the week, and buy what you need to make them.

2 Plan what you're going to cook the night before, and take the meat out of the freezer. Also check and see what ingredients you may be missing.

3 "Shop" your pantry (including freezer and fridge). See what you have, what you really need, what you can make do with, without going to the food store.

4 Go to the grocery store at "off" times like early morning or late at night. I like Wednesdays, as stores tend to be less crowded.

5 Buy enough to make two meals.

6 Don't walk down the junk food aisles. If you don't see it, you won't buy it.

7 Buy in bulk, and re-package and freeze in smaller quantities.

8 If you go to the market more than once a week, only go to buy fresh veggies, fruit, and dairy.

9 Label what you put in the freezer.

10 Be aware of what prices are at the various markets near you. That way you can know when a deal's a deal.

Being organized means you can "shop" your pantry.

You may cook it, but let your child make his/her own food decisions.

5 p.m. when your teenage neighbor can watch your kids. It's called life. And I know it's crazy busy. But if you plan—and start day by day— you *can* figure it out/make it work.

Look at your calendar. Think about what works and what doesn't in terms of leftovers, freezer meals, etc. Ask yourself: What can you make double of to carry over for another night? Or what can you defrost from the freezer that will give you enough time to take Kid #1 to his soccer practice and Kid #2 to her dance class? Plot as best you can how you can compromise schedules, carpools, etc., to get dinner on the table with as much ease as possible.

Maybe that means that on the nights when you have a bit more time, you spend

Mom Tip

"In my freezer always: Perdue® single packet chicken breasts. I put a frozen packet in the fridge every night before bed so it's thawed for dinner. I then flavor with BBQ or toss with bread crumbs. I also love steam-fresh vegetable bags."
—Tara Bucci, Philadelphia, PA
mom of one, 17 months old,

part of it preparing for later in the week, or cooking a big item that can purposely be used for leftovers. Remember: Cooking is not always the answer. Picking up prepared foods or adding sides to a store-bought rotisserie chicken is fine. It's more about getting everyone to the table.

And if it doesn't work out one week? It's nothing to feel guilty about. The mere fact that you're trying—and thinking ahead—is a step in the right direction.

✔ **Be a smart shopper.** You go into a grocery store. You buy. You check out. What's the big deal? The big deal is, just like anything in life, a lot goes into the psychology of a store's layout to entice you to buy more than you need, as well as things you don't need at all. Often, on-

Dinner is do-able if you plan ahead of time.

sale items are displayed at the front of the store or at the end of aisles known as end caps. Don't assume that these items are actually a bargain, since the manufacturers or distributors of these products are often paying for this prime position.

Paying with cash keeps you on budget.

Make sure you have your list, and stick to it. Avoid putting other things in your cart that catch your eye, especially non-food items. Supermarkets want to take advantage of people buying things they did not intend to purchase, so be a smart shopper. It also goes without saying: Never shop when hungry. This is when you'll be most tempted to make poor choices and buy higher-priced items. If you must, eat an apple or banana, sip a cup of coffee, or put a mint in your mouth as a way to calm your cravings before you go shopping. You should also dress warmly, as most supermarkets are often cold. The cold temperature actually makes you hungry, so you buy more. I keep a sweatshirt in the back of my car and always throw it in my shopping cart.

✔ **If you can, bring cash rather than a credit card.** It's a great way (though not always realistic) to buy only what you intend to spend. That, or use your debit card.

✔ **Identify deals in the sales circular before shopping.** Do your homework before you head to the store. Consider coupons and promotions. Get the kids involved as a way to help with reading and math. Many young ones even enjoy the cutting. Wrap coupons around your method of payment so you don't forget to use them.

Comparison shop, and pay attention where you look in aisles.

Mom Tip

"*Freezing fruit is the best. It lasts ten times longer than regular fruit and, when on the go, stays cold and ready when time for a snack at the park.*"

—Shay Pausa, Scottsdale, AZ, mom of two, ages 7 and 10

✔ **Shop the perimeter.** The outer edges of the store are where the healthy foods are, such as fresh fruits, veggies, fish and poultry, and dairy items. Buy fruits in season. The center aisles are where more of the processed products are found.

✔ **Read the labels.** For healthier choices, look for "100 percent" on the label; e.g., 100 percent whole grain or 100 percent fruit juice. Foods with more than five ingredients tend to be more processed. Often, the first three are enough. And avoid artificial ingredients. Not sure which ones are artificial? It's often those you can't pronounce.

✔ **Stay away from foods with cartons that target kids.** They may look fun, festive, and appealing on the outside, but those packages are high in sugar and highly processed on the inside.

✔ **Comparison shop.** Bulk may appear cheaper at first glance, but it's not always so. Compare sizes (e.g., price per oz.) to make sure you're getting what you're paying for. And always ask yourself if you really need whatever you're buying!

✔ **When in the aisles, look up or below.** Grocery stores will often place the higher-priced national brand items at eye level, where your eye naturally goes. But if you look up to the top, or towards the bottom of the shelf, you can spy potential bargains.

✔ **Go with store brands.** Especially for staples such as flour, salt, pepper, etc., store brands are often 20 percent cheaper and the same as, if not better than, some of the national brands. Often, there's no difference other than price and packaging. Don't believe me? A 2009 study by *Consumer Reports* reported that store brands cost up to 27 percent less than national brands, with a taste that's just as good. The reality? When you buy brand-name cheese, you're often paying for the research, development, and marketing costs that go into this household name. With that extra spending on their part comes more cost on your part. The other surprising fact that national brands don't want you knowing: Many products are made

Mom Tip

"Cookbooks written especially for kids have tasty, easy recipes. If you make chicken, fish or pork for your main dish you can change the side dishes to keep things interesting. Once you have a collection of favorite recipes memorized you can easily tweak them with new spices or accompaniments and that helps from your meals becoming boring."

—Diane Asyre, St. Louis, MO, mom of three, ages 10, 12 and 13.

Support a Local Farmer

Want to have organic, fresh-from-the-farm produce and meats delivered practically to your doorstep? Join a CSA (Community-Supported Agriculture). Buy a share, and each week a selection of seasonal fruits, vegetables, and (if selected) meats and poultry will be delivered to a pick-up site in your area. For more information and to find a participating farm, go to GreenPeople.org.

To make sure what you're buying is really packed with the proper nutrients, you need to read the top five ingredients on the label.

Mom Tip

"We all know it, but it cannot be emphasized too much—freeze seasonally. My current favorites are blueberries and whole tomatoes. The key is to freeze clean, dry and loose, on a cookie sheet. Then package, either in a freezer bag or with a vacuum packer, so the items, especially berries, do not freeze in clumps."

—Laura Tabacca, Oxford, OH, mom of two, ages 3 and 4

by the same supplier. Many big-name companies, like Del Monte, McCormick, and Hormel, also make items under store-brand banners (something not advertised). If your hubby is a food snob, do a taste test at home, and see if he notices the difference with his cereal/bread/cookies/you name it—just hide the box.

The other trick to know that what you're getting is just as good: Check the labels. If the first five ingredients are similar or the same between the brands, then most likely you won't taste a difference. Sometimes it's simply a matter of extra salt or water, or even extra chocolate, and who can argue with extra chocolate? Think about it: You trust Trader Joe's, and that's a private brand. My sister, Ann, swears by Whole Foods items.

And if you're like me, a Target aficionado, you trust Archer Farms, that company's food brand. And don't even get me started on Costco's Kirkland Signature brand: I love it! So why not try Stop & Shop, Wegman's, Safeway, or Stater Bros.—whatever brand your local supermarket carries? The other bonus: Because these items "belong" to the store, the retailer generally offers money-back guarantees and/or a full refund.

✔ **Stockpile items when the price is right.** Buy in quantity when you see a sale on your staple items, keeping the seasons in mind. Things like soda, ketchup, hot dogs, and chips are on sale quite often during the warmer months when everyone is cooking on the barbecue. Similarly, things like baking ingredients and canned goods are on sale during the winter months.

✔ **Be aware of costs.** Some grocery stores fluctuate their prices depending on the neighborhood, meaning you can often find a deal by driving a few miles more up the road. My friend, Lynn, stopped going to the Stop & Shop closest to her home when, after picking up her daughter in a neighboring town, she found the same cereal, paper goods, and meats at upwards of 15 percent less at a Stop & Shop 12 miles away.

✔ **Keep your receipts.** If after shopping you discover that the store or another store has the products you purchased

Save Money on Organics

● **Go with store brands** such as Whole Foods Market's 365 Organic Everyday Value, Safeway O Organics, Stop & Shop's Nature's Promise, Trader Joe's and Kroger's Private Selection. Costco's private-label Kirkland Signature organics are often 20% less, compared to the leading national brands.

● **Join a food co-op.** These are independent grocery stores that usually offer local and organic foods. Some have a membership fee; others may require members to volunteer at the co-op for a few hours. Either way: You get a discount when you shop. To find one near you, go to CoopDirectory.org or LocalHarvest.org.

● **Search the web for coupons.** And prioritize your purchases.

fyi

Many snack foods and beverages have added sugar. These foods tend to be low in vitamins and minerals, and the calories add up quickly. Also, drinking calorie-containing beverages may not make you feel full.

Mom Tip

"My must-haves in my pantry are sour cream or plain yogurt (I use them interchangeably), eggs, butter, milk, olive oil, chili powder, brownie mix, canned beans, cream of chicken soup, boneless skinless chicken breasts and hamburger."

—Julie Eddington, Broken Arrow, OK, mom of five, ages 13 to 25

advertised at a lower price, go back and ask for a discount. Don't be shy. Your local supermarket wants to keep you as a customer and will often comply by giving you your money back—with perhaps an extra coupon for a return visit.

Making Sense of Food Labels

Reading and deciphering the nutrition label on the box of cereal, or anything else for that matter, can feel akin to reading *War and Peace*... especially when you're crazy busy rushing through the aisles trying to pick up dinner. Yet, they're important, as they provide you with a detailed look at what's inside the food you and your family are eating. Once you can tell at a glance what's healthy, and what's not, you can make better decisions about the foods you buy and prepare.

The Food and Drug Administration (FDA) and the Department of Agriculture (USDA) require that all food labels show uniform nutrition and health information. But it's often not as easy to understand as it sounds. There's "natural" versus "organic," "low-fat" versus "light." What's a mom to do?

There's the long answer and the short. Since I know that you, like me, are time-pressed, I'm offering the short answer. Though certainly, if your family has specific health issues or you have real concerns, you should check in with your child's doctor or nutritionist.

Start with the ingredients list, basically what foods, spices, and possible chemicals are in the food, and pay attention to the order. Ingredients are listed in order by weight, meaning the first five tend to make up the bulk of the product. Since I'm always in a rush, I tend to go with the first three, as they tell enough of the story.

You want to avoid any foods that have fat, oils and sugars, or any derivatives of these ingredients, listed first. If the first ingredient is one you can't pronounce or have never heard of, chances are it's a chemical or an unnatural ingredient. If you see sucrose, dextrose, molasses, fructose, or high-fructose corn syrup listed first, skip it. Hydrogenated soybean oil, hydrogenated vegetable oil, palm oil, or partially hydrogenated soybean oil are equally as bad, as are colored dyes like blue or yellow. You don't have to be a nutritionist to figure out that if it comes in neon green and bright purple or another unnatural color, you should probably pass.

Check the serving size. This provides you with a quantity telling you how much of this food is equal to one serving (for example 1/2 cup = one serving). The serving size influences the number of calories and nutrients you're ingesting with each serving you consume. Ideally, any serving of whatever size, should be 14 grams of sugar or less to make it a decent food.

Ignore the calories, unless you're looking for you. Granted, that might not be the politically correct advice you're looking for but, personally, I don't think this is a place you need to go overboard dissecting when you have growing toddlers and school-age kids. Yes, I know childhood obesity is on the rise and, yes, I know America's youth needs to eat healthier, but if your kids don't

An "average" fyi

- 40% of calories should come from carbohydrates.

- 30% of calories should come from fat, with most fats coming from sources of unsaturated fats.

- 30% of calories should come from protein.

Also important to know (if you really want to get into it):

- If a food has a daily value of 5% or less of a nutrient, it is considered to be low in that nutrient.

- A food is a good source of a nutrient if the percent daily value is between 10% and 19% .

- If the food has 20% or more of the daily value, it is considered an excellent source of that nutrient.

"Toddlers develop picky food habits, and it really helps for them to see you eating the same food as them. If you make their meals and don't eat with them, it is hard to reinforce that the food is good. They are little imitators, so you have to take advantage of that."

—Kameron Scampoli, Providence, RI , mom of a two-year-old and an infant

have a weight issue or if serious weight issues don't run in your family, I don't think you need to spend a lot of time here, until later into the teen/young adult years. Kids are growing. Pudgy kids become tall, slim teens. As long as you teach them how to eat healthy, the calories shouldn't be an issue.

For the record, though, if you are checking calorie levels, calories give you a measure of how much energy you're getting from a serving. Remember, however, that the number of servings you consume determines the number of calories you actually eat. So if you have two servings of a food, you will have to double the calories listed per serving size to know how many calories you've consumed. On average, 40 calories is low, 100 calories is moderate, 400 calories or more is high.

Make sure what you're giving your little ones is as healthy as you think by double-checking the label.

Cheat Sheet for Reading Labels

For the nitty-gritty on food facts, go to the the Food and Drug Administration's website, fda.gov.

❏ **Read the entire label.** If you focus on only one part, like calories or vitamins, you may not be getting the full story, like how much sugar or fat is in the product.

❏ **Choose foods with a shorter ingredient list.** The more ingredients, the likelier the product is to be higher in calories. If the first three aren't nutrient-rich foods, move on.

❏ **Watch out for added sugars.** High-fructose corn syrup, the most common sweetener of the bunch, is a cheap form of sugar found in everything from juices and flavored yogurt, to nutrition bars and peanut butter. But sugar also travels under the monikers of honey, molasses, corn syrup, evaporated cane juice, fruit-juice concentrate, and malt. If you have to choose, go for something that is "sweetened with sugar" over something that has high-fructose corn syrup.

❏ **Where you can, avoid anything hydrogenated, the fancy name for trans fats, which are made by adding hydrogen to vegetable oil.** These cheap, man-made fats have been linked to an increased risk of heart disease and are frequently found in baked goods and snacks. Instead, focus on monounsaturated and polyunsaturated fats. Found in fish, seeds, nuts, avocados, olives, and olive oil, these fats actually help to lower bad (LDL) cholesterol levels and raise good (HDL) cholesterol.

Need to Know Websites

Put these in your favorites:

* The food-labeling rules set by the U.S. Food and Drug Administration (FDA) are constantly changing. For the latest, go to their website: FDA.gov/Food/Labeling Nutrition/Consumer Information/ucm078889.htm

* Also check out MyPyramid. gov for menu planning, food safety, cooking tips, raising a healthy eater, and other useful information. There's even an interactive computer game for kids ages 6 to 11.

* Want the latest on food safety? Go to FoodSafety. gov which includes recall and contamination alerts, as well as tips on how to safely handle food.

Percent Daily Value shows you the amounts of nutrients an average person will get from eating one serving of that food. For the purposes of food labels, the government has defined an "average" person as someone who needs 2,000 calories a day. So if the label on a particular food shows it provides 25 percent of vitamin D, that 25 percent is for a person who eats 2,000 calories a day. It's hard to speak averages here, which is why I'm not going into major detail—and again, I don't think this is an area you need to spend a lot of time on. What is best for your child is something you and your pediatrician should discuss and determine, keeping in mind that growing tweens and teens, especially those who are very athletic, will need more than 2,000 calories a day.

A little fat is OK. Although eating too much fat can lead to obesity and health problems, growing children need fat as an energy source and to provide insulation and cushioning for the skin, bones, and internal organs. Fat also helps the body to store certain vitamins. Total fat, usually measured in grams, shows how much fat is in a single serving of food.

A good rule of thumb for keeping to the 30 percent calories from fat rule is to check the label and choose foods that have less than seven grams (Denver, Colorado-based nutritionist Julie Hammerstein tells me less than seven grams because some low-fat salad dressings and dairy products are best if they have a little more fat because then they usually have less sugar.)

Some fats are better than others. Unsaturated fats, which are found in vegetable oils, nuts, and fish, are often called good fats. That's because they don't raise cholesterol levels like saturated fats and trans fats do. Both saturated and trans fats are considered bad because they can increase a person's risk for developing heart disease.

Saturated fats usually come from animal products like cheese, meats, and ice cream. Trans fats are naturally found in these foods too, but they are also in vegetable oils that have been specially treated (hydrogenated), so they are solid at room temperature—like shortening. Less than 10 percent of calories should come from saturated fats, and try to keep trans fats less than one percent of your daily calories.

Avoid the hydrogenated or trans fats found in commercially prepared foods such as cookies, cakes, cereal bars, and crackers. Basically these fats are derived from a liquid vegetable or corn oil (the ones that are nearly void of nutrients) and are put through a chemical process that turns the liquid into a solid. This solid form of fat is then added to foods to ensure a longer shelf-life.

These trans fats add no nutritional value to food. Period. And when eaten as part of a daily diet, they are known to increase your risk of heart disease and cancer. Bottom line: Cut out the trans fats, and moderate the healthy fats.

Compromise and a well-balanced diet are key. If you're active, and your kids are active, then some days more junk is allowed; other times you know to watch out for the cholesterol or fats. Just be aware. It's important to teach your kids healthy eating habits.

fyi

DO NOT BUY HIGH-FRUCTOSE ANYTHING!

Mom Tip

"We write out a dinner menu based on our weekly events—complete with meat, starch, vegetable, dessert—along with the page number and name of the magazine/recipe book we have found for new recipes. This also is crucial for shopping. Lists based on the weekly menu are an absolute must. Not only do you not overbuy, you buy what you need for the recipes so that you're not running out at the last minute for ingredients.

Additionally, if we use a recipe from a book/ magazine, we always write the reviews right there in the book."

—Colleen Reynolds, Fort Myers, FL, mom of two, ages 10 and 15

Keeping healthy snacks around the house is an easy way to get your kids eating more fruits and veggies.

Did you know?

- 88% of juices exceed the recommended sugar threshold, and 23% contain high-fructose corn syrup.
- More than 75% of white bread products contain high-fructose corn syrup.
- Go to Good Guide.com for more information.

Look at vitamins and minerals. At this point in your family's life, you want nutrient-dense foods: Ideally those packed with dietary fiber, vitamin A, vitamin C, calcium, and iron. Foods to limit include anything high in fat, cholesterol, and sodium. General rule for fiber is two to four grams per serving.

Natural is not organic. Natural means it is more natural in its composition: It is not chemically produced. Organic is more about how something was raised or grown. Organic is now a regulated industry and means something was raised or grown without pesticides and was fed organically raised food.

Low-fat, no-fat, and light are not the same. When you buy non-fat, you are not buying low-calorie because they replace fat with loads of sugar. Read the label of your favorite

Beware Tricks of the Trade

Despite the labels out there, it's easy to be fooled into thinking that what you're buying is healthier than it is, thanks to misleading words and advertising tricks. Which is why, O'Fallon, Illinois-based dietitian Laurie Beebe stresses knowing where to look. Her tips:

Myth: Peanut butter is not necessarily healthier if it says cholesterol-free.

Reality: Cholesterol is only found in animal products. That means fat in peanut butter of any brand does not contain cholesterol. Does this mean peanut butter is heart healthy? Well, it's still quite high in fat; usually fat comprises more than 75% of the calories in a serving. So the consumer who's looking for something healthy may choose one brand of peanut butter over another because one says cholesterol-free on the label. This implies that other brands are less healthy and may contain cholesterol, when in fact, they don't.

The best peanut butter brands for kids have sugar farther down on the label, as opposed to being one of the first ingredients. Some contain honey and/or jelly, and these would be best avoided also.

Myth: A drink with an ingredient panel that reads "contains 100% real fruit juice" sounds preferable to one that admits it has water and flavors mixed in with small parts of juice concentrates.

Reality: "Contains 100% fruit juice" just means there is real fruit juice within the cocktail. Yes, it's in there, but there are also water, flavoring, and maybe even sugars added. The final product may be just 10% actual fruit juice. You also need to watch out for pear juice concentrate and other concentrated juices that are basically used to sweeten. These concentrates are used more as a sweetener rather than what you assume are really vitamins.

The best juices for kids are those that say "100% juice" as opposed to one that "contains 100% juice."

Beware Tricks of the Trade

Myth: Wheat bread is whole wheat bread.

Reality: Check the first ingredients carefully. For true whole wheat bread, you want to see whole grain flour listed first. But what you often find instead is enriched white flour. Bread that says wheat often implies its whole wheat—some companies even use fluffy white bread to appeal to consumers who like this softer texture and add caramel coloring so it looks like the healthy whole wheat bread. Manufacturers get away with calling this wheat bread when it's what most people call white bread because the grain that is used is wheat!

The best breads for kids are those that have whole grain flour listed first.

Myth: Cereals are healthy and don't have as much sugar as they did in the old days.

Reality: The manufacturers know consumers are savvy shoppers and read the ingredient panel. Which is why, though you'll often see flour listed first, you then see all the various types of sugars broken down; i.e., cane sugar, brown sugar, corn syrup, honey. Though it sounds like flour composes the bulk of the ingredient list, the truth is that the combined sugars outweigh the content of flour by weight. The worst offenders: Frosted cereals or those with marshmallow or candy bits in them.

The best cereals for kids: Those with whole grain or flour and only one or two sweeteners.

Bottom line: Don't just believe what you see on the front of the label; e.g., contains real fruit juice! This is advertising and meant to make you buy. Instead, look at the ingredients and the order they're in. Pick up another product that is similar, and see what the difference is in the ingredients and nutrition facts. The first few comparisons may take some extra time and effort, but once you know what your best choices are, you'll be back to shorter shopping trips, as well as a grocery cart full of healthier food.

Go to MyCoachLaurie.com for more tricks and information.

Eliminate the Dirty Dozen

I switched to organic veggies when my then 11-year-old complained to me that her friend Augusta's carrots tasted better than ours. That's because ours were the pre-cut, pre-sliced short stubby kind that come in plastic bags, while Augusta's mom, Beatrice, always bought organic (meaning they need to be peeled and have the green shoots hanging off the end). And since I wanted Sydney to eat her veggies, I switched. What I learned in the process: There are 12 fruits and vegetables that can slash your pesticide exposure by 90 percent. (It's also a good idea to consider organic when purchasing frozen or canned fruits and vegetables on this list.) Go to FoodNews.org for a guide to pesticides in produce.

- ✘ Apples
- ✘ Bell peppers
- ✘ Celery
- ✘ Cherries
- ✘ Imported grapes
- ✘ Nectarines
- ✘ Peaches
- ✘ Pears
- ✘ Potatoes
- ✘ Red raspberries
- ✘ Spinach
- ✘ Strawberries

non-fat dressing, and you'll see that it's loaded with sugar, typically listed as the first ingredient in the form of high-fructose corn syrup. According to Denver, Colorado-based nutritionist and mom, Julie Hammerstein, it doesn't necessarily make it healthier just because it's low-fat. In fact, it makes it less healthy because we need fat in our diets for hormonal health, cellular function, heart health and a host of other life-giving benefits. Instead, opt for low-fat dressings with less than seven grams of fat per serving (which is usually two tablespoons), and focus on oils such as sunflower seed and olive oil rather than vegetable or corn oils.

Children under two need whole-fat dairy products, so steer away from no-fat. After

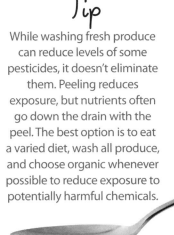

Tip

While washing fresh produce can reduce levels of some pesticides, it doesn't eliminate them. Peeling reduces exposure, but nutrients often go down the drain with the peel. The best option is to eat a varied diet, wash all produce, and choose organic whenever possible to reduce exposure to potentially harmful chemicals.

What "Use-By" and "Sell-By" Labels Really Mean

"Use By":

Food is no longer acceptable and should not be purchased to be used after the given date.

"Use Before" or "Best If Used By":

This means that food may begin to lose quality but still may be used safely. Often used most with frozen foods, cereals, pasta, rice, canned food.

"Sell By":

This refers to the last day that a particular item should be sold, but can be used safely for one week past the "sell-by" date; e.g., dairy and fresh bakery products.

about age six, it's a good idea to find lower-fat dairy products like 2 percent milk, part-skim mozzarella, low-fat yogurt, etc., to replace whole milk dairy products. But don't go for fat-free salad dressings and "fake fat" chips that are replacing all the fat with some chemical substitute.

Again, read the labels carefully. Often, when people shop looking for non-fat foods, they end up spending too much time focusing on what not to eat, rather than focusing on getting calories from naturally low-calorie foods like fruit, vegetables, and lean protein. Because the labels on salad dressings, crackers, cookies, etc., say non-fat, it does not mean that they are always lower in calories.

Listen to Grandma. It's worth repeating. All the vitamins and minerals you need are in fresh foods: Fruits, vegetables, whole grains, nuts, and lean sources of protein. You don't need to read the label for an apple to know that it's loaded with goodness. When you make smart choices, it's less about reading labels and more about eating foods that are naturally loaded with nutrients.

For a quick guide on nutritional information, check out Julie's DVD series, "Max's Minutes—The A-Z's of Healthy Living," at MaxsMinutes.com.

4

What's for Dinner?

How many times have you spent $100 at the grocery store and then ordered pizza because nothing in your eco-bags actually constituted a meal?** Or, what about that time when you picked up Junior from a friend's house, only to hear him say, "Why don't you cook like Matthew's mom does?" "I don't know," you think as you glide past McDonald's drive-through window *again*.

Before I decided mealtime was sacred in my house, I would become insanely stressed by those three little words: "What's for dinner?" By the time I'd get home from work and finally had a chance to start thinking about a dinner menu, everyone—myself included—would be so hungry and cranky that I'd end up ordering in, or reaching for yet another batch of chicken nuggets to throw in the microwave. But when the guilt of serving less-than-nutritious meals—and the expense of last-minute take-out—finally caught up with me, I had no choice but to start putting more thought into dinnertime. And that's when I became an advocate for weekly meal planning.

Mom Tip

*"How do you top a good ol'
Baked Potato? Let us count
the ways!· Salsa + Low Fat
sour cream · Vegetarian Chili·
Marinara sauce and parmesan
cheese· Ground turkey mixed
with taco seasoning, olives
and tomatoes, and topped
with low fat shredded cheddar·
Steam veggies with olive oil
and herbs· Think "repurpose":
last night's rotisserie chicken,
shredded, mixed with sau-
téed diced onions and green
peppers; crumbled meatloaf;
chicken fajitas; sloppy Joes"*

—Meredith Myers, Denver, CO,
mom of two, ages 12 and 8

note to self

When planning your meals,
select recipes that use
healthy cooking methods
like stir-frying, baking,
steaming, and stewing. All
of those methods preserve
the nutrients in your food,
whereas methods like frying
and boiling can let vitamins
and minerals escape.

The truth is, I always found time to plan ahead in my work life—I would never go to a meeting unprepared or fail to meet a deadline. At home, I found, mealtimes required the same kind of attention. That doesn't mean adding hours of labor to your already-busy schedule. All you have to do is figure out a template for your week, a process that should take an hour-and-a-half at most, less as you get used to doing it. It's as easy as thinking about your schedule: Which evenings will you be gone? Which nights can you cook? Putting those details on paper is the first step towards stress-free meals.

By knowing what my family is going to eat a week ahead of time, I know exactly what I need to buy at the store, and I avoid buying food that my family won't eat, therefore cutting down on unnecessary waste. It also gives you a gauge on what your family is consuming and what menu items you might re-work given individual health and dietary needs. Plus—and here's the kicker—imagine how easy it will be for the rest of your family to come up with menus or meals for themselves on those nights you can't be home for dinner. (Hello girl's night out!)

Of course, the biggest benefit of all is that the nourishment of your children and the importance of sitting down together as a family rank high on your priority list, as they should. Call me a late bloomer, but after making a few easy changes, I finally see the light. Here's hoping you will, too.

The benefits:

✱ It helps you figure out what to buy at the grocery store.

* It helps you make a decision on the week's plans, when/if you have time to cook, what older kids can maybe help/prep with and, of course, what you can pull out of the freezer to prepare.

* It means less food spoilage and, hopefully, healthier meals as you figure out what you want rather than scrambling at the last minute to figure it all out.

* Meal planning also works for breakfast, lunch, and snacks. Once you get the hang of it, you'll find you're spending less time in the kitchen and more time with your family.

* Even if you don't stick to it 100 percent, you'll feel more organized and less stressed about mealtimes simply by having it in place.

Hatching the Plan

Here's where flexibility and realism come into play. *This is meant to be a tool to help you, but does not have to be written in stone.* It may change as your plans change. And that's okay, because that's how family life goes. Here, tips to get started:

✔ **Go digital.** Write down all of your family's favorite dishes and store them in your computer. Think about your main dishes (some kind of protein, such as poultry, beef, pork, fish, or soy) and go from there to create meals that fit your family's dietary requirements and

Six Strategies to Stretch What You've Got

❶ Roast a whole chicken. Eat for one meal and make chicken salad, a chicken-and-rice casserole, or chicken tacos with the leftovers.

❷ Grill or sauté extra chicken breasts. Mix with pasta, freeze a portion, or add to stir-fry for another dish.

❸ Buy the supersave-size chicken thighs package. Freeze in smaller quantities. Later, put in a stew or soup.

❹ Make a brisket; with the leftovers, make a salad, add horseradish for a sandwich, or simply add to pasta for a "brisket ragout."

❺ Roast a turkey; with the leftovers, make turkey chili, a turkey Reuben sandwich, or turkey enchiladas.

❻ Buy lots of tomatoes; make tomato sauce with veggies and freeze. Ideally, make with summer veggies for a real treat come wintertime.

SOURCE: IRIS FEINBERG, ATLANTA, GA-BASED MOM OF FOUR AND CO-OWNER OF MAMASAYS (MAMASAYS.US)

Money Saving Tips:

- **Make your own bread once a month, and keep it in the freezer.** One mom I know found a bread machine at a garage sale, and her family is now hooked on homemade bread.

- **On the flip side, buy day-old bread.** Freeze it. It will still be good when you defrost it.

- **Think outside the box.** Go to an international or ethnic market to stock up on rice and spices. They're often less pricey, not to mention it's a fun new shopping experience.

- **Outside the box also means reconsidering the cut of meat a recipe may call for.** If you're going to slice it up or shred it, there's no need to buy the most expensive cut (such as boneless chicken breast). Go for the less expensive cut.

- **Consider substitutions.** Do you really need the brand-name sugar when the store-brand sugar is just as good, but most likely cheaper? Research proves that consistently buying store brands saves up to 20 percent off your weekly grocery bill. If you add it up, it could equal $2,000 at the end of the year..

- **Follow the 2+2 Rule:** Combine two leftovers with two new ingredients to create a quick, easy meal without running back to the store.

- **Start planting.** Grow a garden (a great way to teach kids about food and involve them in the process) or at least some herbs on your kitchen windowsill. You'll save money, plus homegrown tastes better.

- **Keep protein frozen in meal-package-ready wrapping.** Knowing you have a little beef, chicken, or fish in the house cuts down on expensive take-out.

- **Ask questions.** Befriend your local store manager or meat or deli counter personnel. Ask when certain items go on sale. Most sales go in six-week cycles.

A windowsill garden is an easy way to teach youngsters about food and involve them in the process of cooking.

Going digital is one way to keep all your family's favorite dishes – and the shopping lists that go with them – in one place.

lifestyle. Choose lean meats, choose to eat more fish and, for vegetarian eaters, substitute meat dishes with soy and main vegetable dishes. Think, too, about side dishes. Be sure you have at least one vegetable in the rotation each night. For best results, two or more types of veggies at each meal are optimal. Your kids may only eat one, but at least you're offering choices. Tell them they have to pick a green or yellow to make it fun.

✔ **Bookmark favorites.** Put your go-to meal planning sites in easily reachable files. Often you can create a recipe box and tag your finds in a way that makes sense for you (e.g., chicken, pasta, or kid-friendly).

✔ **Consult family members for their thoughts**—trying to get them to stretch beyond their usual pizza and hot dogs. Assign each day a food category or a theme to help you brainstorm ideas.

✔ **Mix it up**, keeping the family budget in mind, adding Dad's favorites, soup and sandwiches, upside-down day (with breakfast for dinner), Mexican night, invite-a-friend-over Fridays, etc., to add variety. Consider *your* needs. If the prospect of cooking the same thing, week-in and week-out, is not motivating, continually work to mix up your list.

Keep your kids happy by asking for their input.

✔ **Check the family calendar for the week.** If you have a lot of activities that will keep you from getting home at a decent hour, you'll want to plan simple meals, leftovers, or take-out for those particular nights.

✔ **Take an inventory of the items in your fridge and pantry.** Do you have any foods that need to be eaten right away? This is one of the greatest benefits of meal planning. You waste much less food because you only buy what you plan on using that week. If you see that you have frozen lasagna or chicken strips and pasta, you know right up front that you have a couple of easy dinners right there and also have less to shop for.

✔ **Consult your recipes.** Recipes are your best friend when it comes to planning healthy meals. You can print out recipes from the internet, many of which can be prepared in an hour or less. To keep organized, keep a three-ring binder on your kitchen shelf as my sister Ann

For example. . .

- ● **Sunday**—pot roast or stew
- ● **Monday**—chicken
- ● **Tuesday**—pasta
- ● **Wednesday**—leftovers
- ● **Thursday**—ground beef
- ● **Friday**—kids' favorites
- ● **Saturday**—Anything goes. . . try a new recipe or opt for dinner out or order in

does. Once you know what's for dinner, you can make a shopping list with the ingredients.

✔ **Consider the seasons.** Shop local and shop the "real foods" (as opposed to processed) that are in season. Not only are they often less expensive, but they taste better and are healthier. Here's where a CSA also comes in handy, as it forces you to use the produce that's available according to the specific time of year.

✔ **Focus on foods that serve more than one purpose.** Eggs continue to be my number-one best example. Sure, they are great for breakfast, but many egg recipes (spaghetti carbonara for one) use eggs for dinner. You can also scramble some, add veggies, and you have a healthy quiche or omelet. Lean ground beef or turkey can add depth to pasta sauces or can easily be made into burgers, tacos, or meatloaf. And cheese, a source of calcium, can add flavor to any dish. Mix them all together for a delicious frittata.

> ## Mom Tip
>
> *"Buy things when you don't need it! Sounds a bit contrarian, but I bought 23 boxes of storage bags and still have some on my shelf. But, this is the week these bags come on sale at their best price of the year, so I stocked up again, saving nearly $3 a box. I don't have to think about buying them again for the rest of the year. Paying attention to sales cycles is helpful so you can stock and save."*
>
> —Julie Parrish, West Linn, OR, mom of three, ages, 6, 8, and 9

✔ **Make your grocery list and check sale items.** Most grocery stores make it easier for you by listing weekly ads on their websites. Most, too, offer printable shopping lists. You can even order online, if that makes life easier. Look for sale items that can be used for this week's meals. If you really want to be frugal, you can plan part of your meals around the items that are on sale, or look for a good deal on the ingredients you need to prepare the dishes you picked.

✔ **Organize your list according to how your supermarket is laid out,** so you're not hopping from aisle to aisle. You'll be less likely to forget something. You'll also be less likely to buy something not on your list, thus saving money and sticking to your budget.

✔ **Think about where you can double up.** Look at where you can buy family-sized packs and double your cooking efforts. Take chicken cutlets, for example. You can prepare some with BBQ sauce, season some for baking, use some for stir-fry, and grill some to use in sandwiches and salads. They'll all be cooked and ready to use as you need them throughout the week. Or, if buying ingredients for lasagna, make two and freeze one. Remember to put everything in a container that can be frozen or heated without needing to change.

✔ **Post your menu on the fridge, and use a standard weekly template.** Opt for a variety of healthy choices, and rotate different types of food throughout the week. Variety is also important in making sure that your body is getting all of the nutrition it needs.

Taking your child to the grocery store is one way to keep her involved in the meal planning process.

✔ **Go international.** Walk the ethnic aisles at your supermarket, or check out a local Asian market for a twist on the tried and true, "same old, same old." Try new kinds of olives in your salad or on your pizza, add zing to burgers with a sprinkle of feta cheese, or experiment with a new kind of noodle for your own variation of Pad Thai.

Here's an example of how to get started.

Weekly Meal Planner

Week of: _Week of February 14th_

SUNDAY

Breakfast: _oatmeal and fruit_
Lunch: _turkey sandwich, chips, apple_
Snack: _celery and carrots with hummus_
Dinner:
    Meat: _pot roast_
    Vegetable: _potatoes and carrots_
    Additional Side: _salad fixings_
    Dessert: _vanilla ice cream_
Notes: _buy bread and fresh salad_

MONDAY

Breakfast: _bagel and cream cheese_
Lunch: _peanut butter, carrot sticks_
Snack: _popcorn_
Dinner:
    Meat: _turkey cutlets_
    Vegetable: _string beans with garlic_
    Additional Side: _vegetable couscous_
    Dessert: _chocolate pudding_
Notes: _double recipe for leftovers on Thursday_

TUESDAY

Breakfast: _cereal with banana_
Lunch: _chicken Caesar salad_
Snack: _soy beans_
Dinner:
    Meat: _ziti- no meat!_
    Vegetable: _salad_
    Additional Side: _garlic bread_
    Dessert: _____
Notes: _____

WEDNESDAY

Breakfast: _yogurt_
Lunch: _vegetable burrito_
Snack: _granola bar_
Dinner:
    Meat: _crock pot chicken_
    Vegetable: _add peas and carrots_
    Additional Side: _____
    Dessert: _cookies_
Notes: _ask kids—rice or potato?_

THURSDAY

Breakfast: _wheat toast with butter_
Lunch: _salad_
Snack: _string cheese_
Dinner:
    Meat: _leftover turkey cutlets_
    Vegetable: _salad or corn_
    Additional Side: _leftover ziti_
    Dessert: _apple pie_
Notes: _PTA meeting tonight. Dine earlier?_

FRIDAY

Breakfast: _waffles_
Lunch: _chicken soup_
Snack: _trail mix_
Dinner:
    Meat: _order in!_
    Vegetable: _____
    Additional Side: _____
    Dessert: _____
Notes: _____

SATURDAY

Breakfast: _eggs and toast_
Lunch: _pizza_
Snack: _banana_
Dinner:
    Meat: _meat loaf_
    Vegetable: _Brussels sprouts_
    Additional Side: _mashed potatoes_
    Dessert: _____
Notes: _cook extra for leftovers next week_

Photocopy these planners and fill them in yourself for an easy way to track your family's meals.

Weekly Meal Planner

Week of: _____

Dinner
for Busy Moms *

*Serving up
Simple Solutions
for Families

SUNDAY
Breakfast: _____
Lunch: _____
Snack: _____
Dinner:
      Meat: _____
      Vegetable: _____
      Additional Side: _____
      Dessert: _____
Notes: _____

MONDAY
Breakfast: _____
Lunch: _____
Snack: _____
Dinner:
      Meat: _____
      Vegetable: _____
      Additional Side: _____
      Dessert: _____
Notes: _____

TUESDAY
Breakfast: _____
Lunch: _____
Snack: _____
Dinner:
      Meat: _____
      Vegetable: _____
      Additional Side: _____
      Dessert: _____
Notes: _____

WEDNESDAY
Breakfast: _____
Lunch: _____
Snack: _____
Dinner:
      Meat: _____
      Vegetable: _____
      Additional Side: _____
      Dessert: _____
Notes: _____

THURSDAY
Breakfast: _____
Lunch: _____
Snack: _____
Dinner:
      Meat: _____
      Vegetable: _____
      Additional Side: _____
      Dessert: _____
Notes: _____

FRIDAY
Breakfast: _____
Lunch: _____
Snack: _____
Dinner:
      Meat: _____
      Vegetable: _____
      Additional Side: _____
      Dessert: _____
Notes: _____

SATURDAY
Breakfast: _____
Lunch: _____
Snack: _____
Dinner:
      Meat: _____
      Vegetable: _____
      Additional Side: _____
      Dessert: _____
Notes: _____

Weekly Meal Planner

Week of: _____

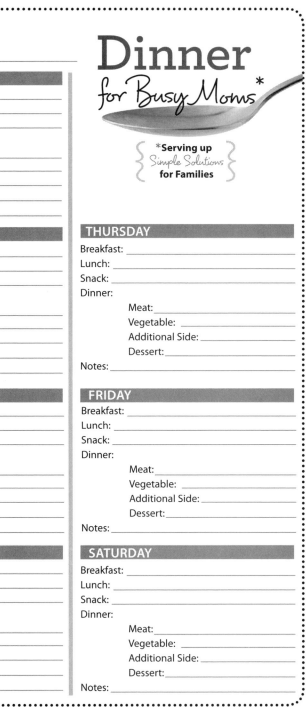

Dinner
for Busy Moms*

*Serving up
Simple Solutions
for Families

SUNDAY
Breakfast: _____
Lunch: _____
Snack: _____
Dinner:
      Meat: _____
      Vegetable: _____
      Additional Side: _____
      Dessert: _____
Notes: _____

MONDAY
Breakfast: _____
Lunch: _____
Snack: _____
Dinner:
      Meat: _____
      Vegetable: _____
      Additional Side: _____
      Dessert: _____
Notes: _____

TUESDAY
Breakfast: _____
Lunch: _____
Snack: _____
Dinner:
      Meat: _____
      Vegetable: _____
      Additional Side: _____
      Dessert: _____
Notes: _____

WEDNESDAY
Breakfast: _____
Lunch: _____
Snack: _____
Dinner:
      Meat: _____
      Vegetable: _____
      Additional Side: _____
      Dessert: _____
Notes: _____

THURSDAY
Breakfast: _____
Lunch: _____
Snack: _____
Dinner:
      Meat: _____
      Vegetable: _____
      Additional Side: _____
      Dessert: _____
Notes: _____

FRIDAY
Breakfast: _____
Lunch: _____
Snack: _____
Dinner:
      Meat: _____
      Vegetable: _____
      Additional Side: _____
      Dessert: _____
Notes: _____

SATURDAY
Breakfast: _____
Lunch: _____
Snack: _____
Dinner:
      Meat: _____
      Vegetable: _____
      Additional Side: _____
      Dessert: _____
Notes: _____

Mom Tip

"We cook big meals on weekends with enough leftovers to last us through a good part of the week. An example:
1. **Spinach lasagna**
2. **Mexican lasagna:** *Tortillas, enchilada sauce, beans, corn, cheese, etc.*
3. **Grilled chicken.** *We'll buy one of those value packs of chicken and grill it all up. On the weekend, we'll have it plain with pasta and some sort of vegetable. During the week, we'll use it in a salad, a quick stir-fry, etc.*
4. **Various pestos.** *My husband's favorite is Poblano pesto served on top or pasta or meat.*
5. **Pot Roast.** *Eat as-is on the weekend, then in a sandwich, using leftovers another day, and then into stew.*
6. **Big pan of roasted veggies, potatoes, and sweet potatoes.** *This provides a hearty side or full meal for several days.*
7. **Black bean burritos.** *We make enough filling to last several meals and then vary the accompaniments. We never seem to tire of these, and they are so easy. We can mostly use canned ingredients, so it's great for midweek rush meals too."*

—Heidi Waterfield , San Francisco, CA, mom of one, age 9

Simple Solutions

Now that your meals are planned, think about how to stretch those meals so you cook once but have enough for the week (or close to it).

✔ **Keep a running food shopping list in a prominent spot in your kitchen, and encourage everyone to add to it.** By sticking to your list, you'll also avoid many of the high-sugar, high-fat, highly processed impulse buys you might normally purchase if you didn't bring a list along.

✔ **Buy family-size packs of protein.** Then prepare cutlets in a variety of ways. You can prepare some with BBQ sauce, season some for baking, use some for stir-fry, and grill some to use in sandwiches and salads. They'll all be cooked and ready to use as you need them throughout the week.

✔ **Double a recipe.** As long as you'll be cleaning those pots and pans anyway, may as well make more than for just one meal. Simply double or triple the recipe, label, and freeze for later use.

✔ **Set aside time.** Over the weekend or one night when you have more time, prepare the meals for the week by doing whatever you can ahead of time. Chop, dice, or cut any vegetable or other ingredients that may be time consuming if you had to prepare it during the week. Store in baggies or containers inside the refrigerator until you're ready to use it.

Crock pot meals are the fairy godmother's answer to a hot (easy!) meal.

✔ **Learn to love your crock pot.** Most moms I know rave about this. They throw everything in the crock pot in the morning and have an amazing home-cooked meal upon their return in the evening. With only one dish to wash in the end!

✔ **Consider casseroles.** Similar to the crock pot, this dish works great with leftovers or just about any items you can find in your pantry. Throw together some pasta, chicken, corn, peas, and potatoes for a quick meal.

✔ **Stick with the classics.** It's great to experiment every now and then, but if you're a busy mom, chances are you don't have loads of spare time to go for the gourmet items. Go easy on yourself: Know that it is OK to regularly serve spaghetti, tacos,

Did you know?

The average parent spends 38.5 minutes per week in meaningful conversation with their children.

SOURCE: A.C. NIELSEN CO.

Want to save money? Look into store circulars for coupons.

Mom Tip

"I love to keep d on hand and have found that it can freeze well. During an illness this year, friends provided us with a meal that has been a quick and easy dinner for our large family is rice pizza. If I have rice frozen, it is easy to take it out the night before or in the morning, let it thaw, spread on cookie sheets, and top with our favorite toppings. Voila! Dinner is ready. I like to make extra rice when cooking it and freeze half of it, saving a couple of steps for a future meal."

—Theresa Gould, Chicago, IL, mom of seven children, ages 18 months to 12 years

homemade pizza, baked potatoes, and soup. Most kids like simple anyway. Your goal is to sit everyone down at the dinner table.

✔ **Use your pantry as inspiration.** With a well-stocked, well-organized pantry, it's much easier to put twists on everyday dishes and improvise on the fly.

✔ **Do prep work in advance.** Enlist your kids to help chop or mix together dry ingredients. You can even start your prep work at breakfast time. It's OK to let certain foods sit on the counter until you get home later.

✔ **Set the kitchen table before you start dinner.** Having a set table helps better prepare you and makes you feel organized. It also sets the tone that dinner will be served at a specific time, and your family's presence is required.

Seven Must-Haves for the Kitchen

To be honest, I get by OK with my sauté pan, cast iron skillet, assorted pots and pans, but those in the know suggest the following and I can't disagree. So, courtesy of Amanda Louden, a mom of two, ages 5 and 7, and a nutritionist based in Gold River, California (go to EatYourRoots.org), here are some suggestions on ways to not only make your life easier, but to keep your food costs down. Hers are the first four; my two cents (meaning the last three) are offered at the end.

❶ **Food processor.** It chops, purees, slices and dices. And it saves time as well as money. You can buy a block of low-moisture mozzarella and send it through the shredder option instead of spending double the cost on pre-shredded packaged cheese.

❷ **Five-to-six-quart crock pot:** Forget those ancient images of mushy meat and cans of condensed cream soup. Crock pots are a great tool for people with busy schedules, or who work long hours. There are crock pots that have a timer and will automatically switch over to the "keep warm" mode after the cooking is done.

❸ **Blender:** A good blender can produce a smoothie better than the local chain, or make a homemade mayo in a matter of seconds. It's versatile and inexpensive.

❹ **Salad spinner:** Not only do salad spinners "spin-out" any moisture from your produce, they double as a fantastic place to store your salad mix in the refrigerator (prolonging the lifespan of the produce). Again:, No need to spend triple the cost for prepackaged salad mix at the store. Instead, simply buy produce, chop, rinse, and spin the remaining water out and then store right in the container. The gap between the basket, which holds the produce, and the outer container, allows any remaining moisture to settle away from the salad. This will allow your salad mix to stay crisp for seven to nine days.

❺ **Good knives and a good cutting board.** Chopping and slicing are always easier with the right equipment. It can be a pain to chop veggies on a tiny cutting board. A large cutting board allows you to keep chopped foods in separate piles while you continue chopping. As for the knives, you can get a nice quality chef's knife for under $30. Keep it sharp, and it will save you a lot of time in the kitchen.

❻ **A countertop grill.** I do hot dogs, hamburgers, grilled cheese, paninis, and enchiladas this way. Also easy for grilling chicken or fish.

❼ **A toaster oven.** My fabulous sister Ann, the cook in our family, taught me the virtues of this one: You can do fries, sides, etc., while you're cooking in the regular oven, and it saves energy to broil sausages/hotdogs/smaller items in there instead of heating your entire large convection oven.

Panko bread crumbs on chicken needs caption.

Mom Tip

"The more veggies are cut, the more flavor you get when you put them in your mouth. That's why a grated carrot gives you so much more satisfaction than just biting into a big old whole carrot."

—Cornelia Zell, Mamaroneck, NY, mom of two, ages 17 and 15, and Pampered Chef consultant, PamperedChef.biz/visitcornelia

✔ **Look for recipes online.** Eventually, your family will get tired of chicken and rice every Wednesday. You can get into a menu rut. Look for new twists on old recipes by following blogs and other sources online. Of course, asking your circle of friends is easiest.

✔ **Store recipes in a central location in your kitchen.** This makes it easy to glance at what you're cooking that week and then what you have in your pantry and need to buy.

✔ **Do your bargain homework.** Clip coupons, read circulars, go to your local store's website. You can save a lot on double or triple coupon days. Plus, if one ingredient is a common denominator in many meals, consider buying in bulk.

✔ **Have breakfast for dinner.** Since breakfast is the most important meal of the day why not enjoy it more than once on occasion? Breakfast can be a goldmine of healthy foods. Go for high fiber cereals, whole grain pancake or waffle mix, fresh fruit smoothies, low fat milk, yogurt, cheese, and eggs.

✔ **Organize for a month.** Sure, it might take a bit longer than your usual routine, but then you're done for a whole 30 days. This is especially helpful when you're anticipating a busy season.

✔ **Plan for leftovers.** Designate one night to be leftover night, and let everyone mix and match whatever's in the fridge from previous nights.

✔ **Go "pre."** To cut down on your prep time, look for precut, prewashed vegetables, fresh fruit, whole grain breads, nuts, beans and quick-cooking lean protein. Frozen vegetables are also great to keep on hand, as well as frozen entrees such as Healthy Choice®, Weight Watchers®, or Lean Cuisine®. Just add a salad or cooked vegetable to round out the meal. I'm also a big fan of Boboli® breads and the Healthy Pantry.

✔ **Have groceries delivered:** Depending on where you live, ordering your groceries and scheduling delivery times are only a click away—a huge time saver! Meal delivery services are another option, with meals packaged and delivered right to your door. Nothing is quicker and easier than a meal that's already prepared, portioned, and ready to go.

Five Ideas for Chicken

❶ **Add to salad.** In our house we love chicken Caesar salad. Shred cooked chicken into pieces and toss with lettuce, breadcrumbs, and Caesar dressing.

❷ **Turn it into a sandwich or a tortilla wrap.** Cut cooked chicken into strips then place in a wrap along with lettuce, grated cheese and tomato with mustard or mayo.

❸ **Throw it in a taco.** Leftover chicken meat is easily converted into a tasty taco filling. All you have to do is cube and heat the meat. Add toppings and place in taco shells.

❹ **Toss with pasta.** If you can boil water, chicken Alfredo is easy to make. Simply boil noodles until they're soft. Top with Alfredo sauce and heated chunks of chicken.

❺ **Sauce it up.** I often marinate chicken breasts in barbecue sauce or a store-bought Italian dressing, or even mustard. For the mustard recipe, I add breadcrumbs and bake. Serve with rice or potato.

Easy Uses for Ground Beef

Here are some ways to get the most mileage out of ground meat:

- **Stir-fry:** Mix with a bag of frozen stir-fry veggies and some soy sauce, serve with rice.
- **Stroganoff:** Mix with a can of creamed soup and a package of dry brown gravy mix, maybe some onions or mushrooms. Serve over noodles.
- **Spaghetti:** Add a bit of sauce and voila! Dinner is served.
- **Curry:** Mix with leftover veggies (or a bag of frozen) and instant curry cubes. Serve with rice.
- **Gravy:** Either make milk gravy, or cheat and use a mix (country or brown) and serve over rice, bread or biscuits.
- **Pot pie/Shepherd's pie:** Combine with a can of mixed veggies, white sauce, or creamed soup. Cook in a casserole dish with either boxed mashed potatoes or biscuits on top.
- **Tacos/burritos:** Add spice mix and serve either on burrito wraps or in taco shells with regular accompaniments.
- **Soup:** Use either broth or tomato juice for base, add veggies and a starch if you like.
- **Hamburger casserole:** Use a starch, like noodles, creamed soup or white sauce, corn and peas, salt and pepper.
- **Hamburger mac and cheese:** Add to your favorite mac and cheese recipe.
- **Chili mac:** Add to cooked elbow noodles, spaghetti sauce, chili powder, beans, onion and green pepper. Bake.
- **Sloppy Joes:** Use your favorite recipe.

REPRINTED FROM JENN FOWLER, AKA FRUGAL MOM (FRUGALUPSTATE.COM)

Easy Dinners—Promise!

It should not surprise you when I tell you that I am not a cook. I can heat up. I can stir, and boil, and even bake. But I'm no Julia Child. I'm also not one of those people who scour recipes—and try new things. I'm easily intimidated by anything that features more than five ingredients and says it takes only 30 minutes. Their 30 minutes is often my 60. Though I love the scent of a hearty beef stew simmering on the stove for hours, and feel strongly that a busy kitchen feels cozier and homier with he aroma of a slow-cooked meal, it's not something I do on a daily basis.

Which presents a challenge because, as my kids have gotten older, and I've tried to expand their palates, I've had a hard time coming up with new recipes to try. The answer? The following fool-proof, under-ten-minutes-to-make dinners.

Under-Ten-Minute Meals

* **Set up an at-home salad bar.** Set out bowls of different toppings and let people choose what they want to put in their salad. Same idea works for baked potatoes.

* **Plan for pizza.** Get a store-bought pizza crust, bagels or English muffins. Top with tomato sauce and shredded mozzarella, and pop in the toaster oven. Dinner in ten minutes! You can also add the topping bar idea above with bowls of veggies, pepperoni, chicken, and beef. Frozen pizza works too.

You can't mess these up!

These are my fave foolproof recipes:

✔ **Crock pot Chicken:** Take four frozen boneless skinless chicken breasts, place in the bottom of a crock pot. Cover with a large can of cream of mushroom soup. Cook on low all day. Serve over rice or noodles, veggies, and garlic bread. The soup makes the best gravy.

✔ **Sweet Salmon:** Brush salmon with a mixture of soy sauce, lime juice, and a touch of honey. Bake until lightly brown.

✔ **Baked Ziti:** Toss cooked ziti with pasta sauce and shredded mozzarella in a casserole dish. Top with more mozzarella and a sprinkle of parmesan. Bake until cheese melts.

✔ **Cuban Chicken:** Brown skinless chicken breast with olive oil, salt, pepper, and garlic powder. (You might want to slice it first or after.) Throw in a can of black beans, and add a little vinegar and sugar, emphasis on little. Make a package of yellow rice according to the directions. Place your rice on the plate, put the bean/chicken mixture on top, and garnish with salsa, depending on your taste. You can also use chicken thighs and legs, depending on what you like.

* **A simple standby: Soup and Sandwiches.** Or just sandwiches. A favorite standby in our house is peanut butter with carrots and apple slices on the slide. It's healthy. It's easy and no one ever seems to tire of peanut butter.

* **Wrap it!** Same premise as your at-home salad bar. Set out bowls of toppings and meats; make sandwiches into wraps. We love guacamole, chopped tomatoes, and ground beef.

* **Prepare pasta.** If your kids are pasta lovers, as mine are, boil noodles and keep some in the fridge for an instant cold pasta dinner. Just top with melted cheese or tomato sauce or add diced chicken, carrots, and maybe some seasoning. It's also a great way to feed picky eaters two different things easily: One pasta princess can have butter sauce on hers; another simple tomato sauce.

* **Make tomato sauce.** Throw together equal parts tomato paste and water, garlic, fresh basil, oregano, salt and pepper, veggies (to sneak in for kids), and ground beef

Seasonal Cooking

As the seasons change, we coordinate our hot- and cold-weather dishes. In the summer we eat more grilled food, stir fries, and lots of fruit and salad. As much as we can, we keep the oven off, the grill fired up, and the microwave at the ready. Some seasonal dish ideas:

Summer

❑ Salads: Chicken Caesar, garden, pasta, potato
❑ Kabobs: Add chicken, pineapple, green peppers, beef, etc.
❑ Anything grilled!
❑ Anything with barbeque sauce!
❑ Fish: Filets, shrimp on the barbie
❑ Sandwiches or wraps. For variety, serve sandwiches open-faced.

Winter

❑ Beef stew
❑ Beef or turkey chili
❑ Meatloaf
❑ Casseroles
❑ Spaghetti and meatballs
❑ Shepherd's pie
❑ Roast beef and mashed potatoes
❑ Baked potatoes with toppings
❑ Chicken in a pot
❑ Soup

Expert Advice: Ellyn Satter's
Mastering Family Meals: Cooking, Planning and Shopping

Cooking, planning, and shopping are big topics. To help you get started, here are some thoughts from *Secrets of Feeding a Healthy Family* by Ellen Satter.

- **Become a fast and thinking cook.** In order to celebrate eating and take good care of yourself with food, you have to cook—and keep on cooking. Plan to cook from scratch, cook using convenience foods and convenient ingredients, or cook ahead and eat leftovers. Yes, you can cook. For a recipe to get you started, check out Tuna Noodle Casserole at EllynSatter.com. Whether you are preparing meals at step two, three, or four, *Secrets* gives you recipes and quick food-preparation tips.

- **Use planning, don't abuse it.** You are using planning when you rough out a menu for the next few days, then take five minutes the night before to check the menu for the next night's dinner, get the canned goods lined up, and put the frozen vegetables toward the front of the freezer. You are using planning when you take shortcuts, and make extra, and use leftovers for another meal. But you are abusing planning when you make your meals complicated and pile on so much work that you can't sustain the effort. You are also abusing planning when you say, "Oh, we shouldn't eat that; it isn't good for us."

- **Consider your shopping strategy.** Think about it, experiment, and find a way of shopping that works for you. Random grocery shopping wastes time, energy, and money, and defeats your cooking endeavors. In *Secrets*, I suggest shopping at three different levels:

  –Every three to four weeks: Big staples shopping. This is a major shopping excursion at a grocery emporium to stock up on foods that keep, such as frozen, canned, bottled, and dry foods, cleaning supplies, and paper goods.

  –Weekly: Produce, dairy, and fresh meat for the week.

  –Quick-stop: Milk, maybe bread or bananas.

Think about what's tops on your list. To take the trouble out of eating and put the joy back in, make feeding yourself and your family a priority.

or turkey. Pour over spaghetti or fettuccini, plus it is easy to freeze. Fettuccine is very versatile; you can change its flavor easily with different veggies, herbs, and proteins.

* **Just add sticks.** Sometimes, just adding fancy colored toothpicks or a kebab to chicken, a sandwich, or turkey makes it more enticing and fun.

* **Dress up potatoes.** Mix three sliced potatoes with fresh veggies and turkey sausage, drizzle with olive oil and seasonings of your choice (try Cajun or Provencal) for a potato veggie grill. Place contents in a covered container safe for microwave cooking and cook on high for 10 minutes.

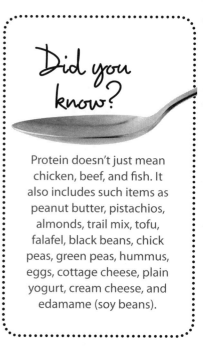

Did you know?

Protein doesn't just mean chicken, beef, and fish. It also includes such items as peanut butter, pistachios, almonds, trail mix, tofu, falafel, black beans, chick peas, green peas, hummus, eggs, cottage cheese, plain yogurt, cream cheese, and edamame (soy beans).

* **Marinade it.** Put chicken in a sealed baggie with your favorite marinade. Refrigerate in the morning; then take out and cook for dinner for a tasty treat. Add couscous (It cooks in less than five minutes.) or a frozen veggie, and you've got a well-balanced meal.

* **Roll it in breadcrumbs.** Panko-crusted. Italian-seasoned. Just a little change of mixture helps change the flavor of chicken/beef/pork.

* **Make quesadillas.** Put a flour tortilla in a grill pan or skillet; add pre-shredded cheese, canned beans, chopped tomatoes, or other veggies; add more cheese, fold it. Serve with salsa.

* **Stir fry.** The basic ingredients are the same each time—chicken, rice, and a mix of vegetables (Keep a bag of frozen mixed veggies on hand if you don't have fresh.) The taste can be altered with various sauces.

* **Use a slow cooker/crock pot**. This is a busy person's dream. Simply set everything up in the morning and enjoy a warm, home-cooked meal when you're through with your busy day.

Stretching Recipes— and Your Budget

I'm forever reaching out to other women— even those I don't know (thanks to the web, it's easy)—which is why, when Silver Spring, Maryland-based Janet Riley, Senior Vice President of Public Affairs at the American Meat Institute (and mom of two boys, ages 9 and 12), sent me these tips, I had to include them. Read them and rejoice: They are simple, out of the box solutions that make for easy ways to save at the grocery store and use meat in ways you might not have thought of.

❶ **Retro Rocks.** Dust off your mom's crock pock and learn to use it to transform economical cuts into tender treats through this moist heat cooking. The classic beef pot roast using the chuck, or the modern pork carnitas using the pork butt, are just a crock pot away.

❷ **Customize Classics.** Burgers are classic, economical meals. Add new flavor by mixing in seasonings like bleu cheese, herbs, or chipotle peppers. Or try a ground lamb burger with Greek seasonings. Buying the lean formulations—like 90 percent lean— offers flavor with less fat.

❸ **Rub It In.** Adding a dry rub to an economical cut like the tender flat iron steak makes a delicious meal that's packed with protein, iron, and other vitamins.

❹ **Dig the Deli.** Popular brands of deli meats offer surprisingly good nutrition at low

Surprise Fact

About 30% of consumers used microwaves to prepare their food in 2008, a 10% increase from figures registered between 1990 to 2007, according to The 24th Annual Report on Eating Patterns in America by The NPD Group. Stove tops remain the most popular cooking appliance, but the percent of main meals prepared on a stove top dropped from 52% in 1985 to 33% in 2009.

Did you know?

You can cook pasta in less than 10 minutes without boiling water, and you can cook vegetables with less water and don't have to wait for the water to boil. Make friends with your microwave.

"One whole chicken can be used for several meals throughout the week. Boil the chicken in a stock pot with enough water to cover. Add salt, pepper, garlic, onion, carrot, and celery. Boil for at least one hour for broth or up to three hours for stock. Strain the liquid, and you've got enough broth or stock for soup or to use throughout the week in other recipes. Remove the chicken from the bones, and use some for chicken pot pie one night and chicken salad for lunch."

—Dawn Viola (DawnViola.com), Orlando, FL-based food writer, and mom of one, age 9

costs. A serving of one major brand of honey ham has 70 calories in a serving, 10 grams of protein, and just 2.5 grams of fat. Add slices of ham to salads and omelets to satisfy while adding good nutrition.

❺ Befriend Your Broiler. Food experts call the broiler the upside down grill. The heat comes from the top, but gravity pulls fat away, offering a healthier way to cook meat indoors. And everybody owns one. It's the perfect way for an apartment dweller to cook healthy.

❻ Sausage is Soooo Savory. Add sausage to pasta or rice dishes for added flavor—or make your own unique version of paella. Check out the nutrition labels on today's sausage products. They're leaner than you think and come in a wide array of flavor profiles, from sun-dried tomato and basil, to mango. And you'll pay far less than you would for a premium cut of meat.

❼ Kabob It. Cuts of meat like sirloin can be tenderized by marinating and threading with vegetables on kabob sticks for a colorful and balanced meal. Summer grilling or winter broiling will whisk fat away and offer a delicious, easy, and slightly exotic entrée.

❽ Dress to Impress. The most basic meals can be made more interesting with salsas and fruit-based chutneys (hello, anti-oxidants). Peach chutney adds flavor and moisture (plus is low in fat) to an economical pork loin without breaking the bank.

5

Feeding Your Family...
Without Becoming a
Short-Order Cook

If dinner were a TV sitcom, the title would most likely be *Suppertime Sagas: It Was The Best of Times... It Was The Worst of Times.* What I mean here is that it can be amazing, as in fabulous conversation, the mixture of aromas and cuisines, and a feeling of camaraderie, warmth, and humor. And it can be horrible, as in silverware clattering, chairs scraping, kids kicking each other under the table (or sneaking veggies to the dog), and conversation at a standstill thanks to screaming/crying (yours *and* the kids). Throw in complaints about the chewy meat, the too-cheesy sauce, or why you didn't separate the chicken from the carrots on the plate because *they are touching*, and you have the modern family's 21st century meal.

The scene changes minute by minute, as well as daily, weekly, monthly, and yearly, depending on what you're serving, how you're serving it, when you're serving it, and the age of whom you're serving it to. (And yes, sometimes it's even the husbands that add to the chaos.) Certainly, dinner with 2- and 5-year-olds looks drastically different than dinner with 10- and 12-year-olds. And through all those ages and stages you worry/wonder/obsess if your kids are getting enough food, getting the right foods, and forming the *right* relationship with food. It is, pardon the pun, all on your plate.

And just another challenge to the mealtime mayhem is *A Mom's Life* (yet another sitcom where you're not sure if you should laugh or cry or both). Playing the part of the difficult child: A 2-year-old who hates anything green, a 5-year-old who will only eat mac and cheese if it's served on his favorite plate, an 8-year-old who insists on eating pasta with butter sauce 24/7, and a 12-year-old who's suddenly decided she's a vegetarian. Or maybe your "episode" includes the tween who's counting calories and refuses to touch half the things you've cooked for dinner, or the teenager who tries to sneak her cell phone under the table to text after she's inhaled a bag of chips and tells you she's not hungry. And then there's you—the starring role of Keeper of the Dinnertime Hour in sweats and a ragged t-shirt after a day's worth of tending to the house and kids, or wearing a skirt and blouse after a stressful hour of dealing with bumper-to-bumper traffic on your way home from your office, trying your best to accommodate your family's needs, get a decent meal on the table, and encourage everyone to sit together in peace for 30 minutes.

Ah, kids. Just as you've gotten your strategies together for figuring out what they'll eat, how they like it served, and when best to serve it (based on everyone's over-extended schedules), your child changes from an adorable baby to a fussy toddler, a grade schooler who no longer likes the same foods she had last week, a tween who's freaked out about her bulging pile of homework and races through her meal

Toddlers are notorious picky eaters, but you can find ways to please them.

Six Simple Rules

❶ Turn off the TV, cell phones, Blackberries, and other electronic devises.

❷ Make the atmosphere nice.

❸ Encourage conversation.

❹ Involve your children. They can mix the salad, set the table, load the dishwasher.

❺ Be a role model.

❻ Pick your battles.

without touching it, and a teen who's upset she's missing face time on Facebook, meaning she doesn't want to talk to you, let alone sit with you. Many times you'll find these stages repeated. Seriously: How many of us look at our 16-year-olds and think they're not all that different from the defiant toddler we once remembered? Indeed, as we moms know from when we were kids, it's a child's job to keep us on our toes.

But today, instead of just setting rules and sticking to them, we parents of the '00s often act like circus performers trying every trick in the book to get our kids to eat. We stand on our heads. We entertain with zoom spoons and funky-shaped nuggets. We sneak in veggies. We bribe with goodies. And we make all sorts of promises, all in an effort to get our children to eat or at least sit at the table without fidgeting. At some point we have to stop obsessing over our little princes and princesses and do what works for *us*.

Unless your kid has a specific medical condition, kids will eat when they are hungry. My mom never offered my sister and me ten different choices before we sat down for dinner. It was what she offered or nothing. And she never hesitated to tell us, after a long day working, carpooling, and slaving over a hot stove, that come 8 p.m., the kitchen was closed.

Restyling the Menu

Williston, North Dakota, mom Maeve MacSteves always gives her six kids (ages 6 to 16) two choices for dinner: Take it or leave it. She's happy to report that the take-its always outnumber the leave-its by 1,000 to 1.

Uber-mom of 14 kids (ages 7 to 33), Shannah Godfrey, of Independence, Missouri,

Save time by chopping and slicing as far in advance as you can.

agrees. Her tactic: Remember who's boss. "You're the parent," she says. "Your kitchen is not a restaurant, and you shouldn't approach your dinners that way. Your kids will adjust to the rules and boundaries you set."

I don't know why, but I always think moms with a lot of children know best. They don't cater to every whim the way moms of one or two or three do. (And I put myself in this category, so don't feel singled out here.) They're more regimented. Their kids are more accountable for their actions.

Expert Ellyn Satter (EllynSatter.com) a therapist, dietitian, and author who developed a model for feeding children based on trust and acceptance known as "The Division of Responsibility in Feeding," feeds into this concept (sorry, couldn't resist the pun) and, frankly, I think more of us should follow her lead. Her philosophy, which she's written about in books, countless articles and on her website, basically states that adults are responsible for what, where, and when children eat, and children choose how much and whether to eat.

It's our job to prepare meals and snacks at regular intervals, make eating together enjoyable, show children acceptable mealtime behavior, and let children grow up having bodies that are right for them. When we trust that our kids can decide how much and whether to eat, they'll eat the amount they need, will learn to eat the foods we eat, will grow predictably, and will learn to behave at the dinner table. They'll also learn to listen to their bodies' signals for hunger and satiety.

Sound like an unattainable goal? It doesn't have to be. It's a fact: Children are born with the innate ability to know how much and when to eat. You see it almost from the minute they're born. An infant will signal when she's hungry by opening her mouth and rooting for the nipple (or crying, if these signals are missed by the parent). When she's full, she'll turn her head away.

My goal here is not to get into the child psychology of eating, but to preserve your sanity and make dinner as easy as possible for *you*. Meaning, there's no reason why you have to continue to be a circus performer, juggling 12 balls in the air just to appease every palette in your family.

And though I believe in flexibility and choices and doing what works for *your* lifestyle, I also advocate putting the brakes on accommodating everyone all the time. After all, you need to

Mom Tip

"Feed kids their favorites. If everyone likes chicken except one, serve chicken. Just be sure that the meal includes at least one item that the non-chicken lover particularly likes. Try spices and ingredients to determine what works for your family. My children would eat carrots if either Italian seasonings and salt, or pumpkin pie spice and a little sugar, were added!"

—Cornelia Zell, Mamaroneck, NY, mom of two, ages 17 and 15

Children are born with an innate ability to signal when they are hungry.

The meals your kids love best are often the ones they help prepare.

Mom Tip

"If you're a non-cook, surrender to the process of becoming a cook. You're not going to be perfect. The food will be awful at first. But it's a process. It gets better."

—Anna Johnson, Oakland, CA, mom of one, age 2

preserve your sanity, for as the old saying goes, "If Mom's not happy, no one's happy."

You *can* enjoy pleasant meals, where everyone eats in peace. At this point, you've sailed through the previous chapters and now have strategies, or at least good intentions. All of which is a step in the right direction.

You have the well-stocked (and healthy) pantry. You have the meal plans. You have the organized shopping lists. And you have the clutter-free table that you or your kids have set for dinner. Now's the easy part (ha!): To get your child to try new things, expand her palate, show off her table manners, and give you something other than a curt "fine" when you ask about her day.

Yes, you will deal with picky eaters. (It's a phase.) And, yes, you'll deal with obnoxious teens. (It's also a phase.) But gradually, your child's eating habits—and mood swings—will balance out, with the dinner table as a backdrop for all these changes. Still using the TV sitcom theme here, it's time, my fellow busy moms, to change the script.

Ages and Stages

Here, age-appropriate tips for how to create an enthusiastic eater...or at least get them to sit with you at the dinner table.

Babies

✔ **By age one, most babies are ready to join you at the table.** Offer foods in a pleasant environment and with a positive attitude.

✔ **Put a couple of pieces of food aside for baby before you add seasonings.** Depending on the age of your child, she might not be ready for something overly spicy.

Let your kids get messy and enjoy the eating process.

Tasty Ways to Start Baby Eating Right

Jennifer Perillo, a mom of two from Brooklyn, New York, and self-proclaimed foodie (she blogs at InJenniesKitchen.com) is convinced that making baby food for her second daughter helped her to become a better eater. Though she didn't set out to feed her second daughter by designing home-cooked foods—it just sort of happened—she says she does notice that baby Virginia has a more appreciative relationship with food than her six-year-old does.

Unfortunately, better tasting baby food costs more, but she says what it costs financially in the short term will often pay off in the long term— meaning you'll have a more enthusiastic eater who is more receptive to flavor and taste.

My two cents, as you know from reading this far, is that moms shouldn't have to feel guilty for what they can't do, and pressure for what they don't have time to do. But (there's always a but, isn't there?) it *is* something to consider, even if it's just a little side dish once a week.

By starting early and introducing homemade baby food, you can shape your child's palate with food that is healthy and delicious. This helps them to learn what fresh foods look, smell, and taste like—and will assist in the transition to table food, advises Connie Pope of Jacks Harvest, a frozen organic baby food company (JacksHarvest.com).

She says she used to mix ¾ mango with ¼ peas (mango was her son's favorite flavor), then gradually adjusted to ½ mango and ½ peas, then ¾ peas and ¼ mango, and eventually 100 percent peas as a way to get her son to eat his veggies. "New flavors shunned at first are often accepted after repeat offerings," she says. "You can add a very small amount of herbs and spices to your baby's food to help build a future reliance on flavors other than salt and sugar. Cinnamon, a powerful antioxidant, is delicious added to pears, apples, peaches, and sweet potatoes. Healthy herbs like mint, which goes great with peas, and ginger, which cooks nicely with carrots, both soothe tiny digestive tracts."

No time to puree or mash? No worries. Check out Happy Baby (HappyBabyFood.com), TastyBaby (TastyBaby.com), and Jack's Harvest (JacksHarvest.com).

Make food fun by making faces on sandwiches or using cookie cutters to create shapes.

✔ **Don't fuss if food is refused.** Simply try again a little later. The important point to remember is that every taste and texture will be new, so repeated exposure to a variety of foods is key.

✔ **Substitute.** If your child continually refuses to eat certain foods, provide others with similar nutrients, e.g., sweet potatoes for carrots, or peaches for pears.

✔ **Don't worry if your baby isn't interested in eating exactly when you are.** Babies have their own schedules and change as they grow. Believe me, he will let you know when he is hungry. It takes a while to get him on *your* schedule.

Toddlers

✔ **Make meals fun by dressing up the usual.** Make a face on a peanut butter sandwich with raisins and bananas, use cookie cutters to make shapes, add a little melted cheese on broccoli, put fruit on a kabob. Or simply put some finger foods in a muffin tin, or other interesting container, and let your child pick out what she wants. Sometimes just mixing up the bowl can entice your child to eat it. When my girls were little, I'd layer cereal in parfait glasses with sliced strawberries and yogurt. For my ice cream lover, Sydney, I'd sometimes put an ice cream cone on top for a fun afternoon treat.

Note to Self

Pack healthy food when you go out to parks and playgrounds. Even the most stubborn non-fruit-and-veggie-eating youngster will eat an apple or orange if they are hungry, especially when the alternative means going home early.

Mom Tip

"We involved our children in kitchen chores since they were able to walk and hold a plastic cup. We started by having them clear their own place. As they grew more capable, we expanded that to filling, putting things back in the fridge, and getting out utensils. Now they know that kitchen duties are a part of what a family does out of respect for one another."

—Diane Asyre, St. Louis, MO, mom of three, ages 10, 12, and 13

✔ **Roll it, dip it, dunk it.** Toddlers are all about the sensory experience. Let them use their fingers to grab and touch, dipping carrots in a yogurt sauce, slices of chicken into applesauce, a strawberry into melted chocolate, even chunks of fruit into honey and then into crushed cereal.

✔ **Let them feed themselves and make a mess.** Children learn from imitation and need to practice self-feeding. It's important to provide finger foods they can put into their mouths by themselves.

✔ **Serve a variety of foods, and encourage your young ones to try new things.** At the very first signs of finicky behavior, explain to your child that it is not healthy to eat the same foods all the time.

✔ **Include them in every aspect of eating,** from shopping to recipe planning to cooking and serving. Children are more likely to eat something they have been involved in, so take them shopping, talk to them about making decisions. Give them a cookbook with pictures, and let them page through it. Have them mark pictures they like with a sticky note, and go back through them together. Explain what the dish is and all of the ingredients. If they still think it sounds OK, make it a part of that week's dinner. Make one night *their* night where they either pick the meal or help to plan it. As they get older, they can even help to cook it. Let them wash the fruit they've selected, put things in the pantry, place napkins on the table, and play chef as they help you in the kitchen.

✔ **Offer choices.** Asking "Do you want broccoli or cauliflower for dinner?" as opposed to "Do you want broccoli for dinner?" gives them a sense of control, meaning they're more likely to go for one option, and you're more likely to get some veggies in them.

✔ **Be realistic.** It is not reasonable to try to force your child to eat a whole serving of food, nor is it likely your little one will sit through a whole meal. Keep your expectations small, like one bite of a new food, or five minutes at the table with everyone, and work your way up from there.

✔ **Be consistent, and don't give up.** Use the same tactics at each and every meal as a way to reinforce the importance of not only trying new foods, but sitting together as a family.

✔ **Don't turn the kitchen into a restaurant.** You can be accommodating to a point, but in the interest of saving your sanity, and getting dinner on the table, it's best to cook one meal for everyone.

✔ **Be patient, and give kids time to eat.** Children feed off of your emotions; if they sense forcefulness or desperation, you may be pushing them away.

✔ **Don't worry if they're picky.** That's normal. It can take up to a dozen tries of a certain food before your child accepts it.

✔ **Introduce a rainbow of colorful foods.** Let your child pick three colors,

A Kitchen Splurge

Kids of all ages love sliders—which is why I love Sur La Table 'Slider' Mini-Burger Tools, an easy way to serve perfectly rounded patties. They're great as appetizers for a party, as a main entree or as a fun way to introduce turkey and veggie burgers. Go to SurLaTable.com for more information.

Mom Tip

"It's fine to present food in a way that kids find appealing, but when it really comes down to it, this just makes it more challenging for the parents. I encourage parents to make the plate as colorful as possible—not a lot of browns and beiges, but use more colors of the rainbow.

Also, remember that too big a serving size can put kids off. They don't need to be eating as much as adults, so put portions on their plate that are as big as the child's fist. A 4-year-old has a much smaller hand than a 14-year-old, so their portions of meat, pasta/grains, and veggies/fruit are going to be smaller. If you put too much food on the plate, and your child doesn't eat all of it, then that sends a negative message, when really some tummies only need four or five bites of each food on their plate."

—Julie Hammerstein,
certified nutritionist,
Denver-based mom of
one, age 7,
(MaxLifeTherapies.com)

and then try a fruit or vegetable representing each. For example, offer some blueberries with yogurt for breakfast, some carrots with lunch, and cherry tomatoes at dinner.

✔ **If they are picky, offer non-food rewards in an age-appropriate fashion.** The younger the child, the more immediate the reward. Offer a 3-year-old a sticker for taking a bite of a new vegetable, but require a 10-year-old to try three new foods before he earns those extra ten minutes of a later-than-usual bedtime. Never offer trips to fast-food restaurants or junk food as rewards, as this teaches them to value the unhealthy foods over the healthy foods. (See more tips for picky eaters on page 142.)

✔ **Don't force your child to eat.** If your child isn't hungry, she's not hungry. However, the family must sit together, and your toddler, with a coloring book and some crayons, can still be engaged.

✔ **Keep serving sizes manageable.** Remember, what may be a serving size to you often is not for your child. Go with the size of the child's fist as a guide.

✔ **Be a role model.** Children's food preferences are largely shaped by what their parents eat. It sends the wrong message if you encourage your child to eat nutritious foods and then reach for a bag of chips and soda on the way out the door. The foods you eat and introduce to your

There's nothing wrong with Mac and Cheese—just don't make it every night.

children early in life help set the stage for a lifelong habit of healthy eating.

✔ **Avoid making only your child's favorites.** Serving mac and cheese, hot dogs, plain pasta, and chicken nuggets to him when he's young ensures he'll expect only those foods when he's older. Offer these foods in moderation.

✔ **Engage your child in conversation.** Don't just talk adult talk. Interact with your child, and make this time of day family time.

✔ **Allocate shelf space.** By making foods and serveware accessible, your child can help herself and choose what she wants. I always kept the bottom drawer in my kitchen for plastic kid-friendly plates so my daughters could grab a plate or cup. This also enabled them to eat when they were hungry, which helped to promote their independence.

Always have two things on the table your kids will like.

Grade School

✔ **Engage your kids in conversation that involves them.** Move beyond the usual "How was school today?" to more inventive ways to get them to open up, such as, "When I was in X grade, I remember doing X, Y, Z. Is that what your teacher does?"

✔ **Graduate from kids' foods.** They should be eating what you're eating. Children learn by example. Encourage them to eat the foods you eat.

✔ **Always have two things on the table you know the kids will like.** It can be as simple as bread and butter or apple slices with peanut butter, or it can be two kinds of vegetables or two kinds of potatoes. (And yes, store-bought sides are welcome.).

✔ **Involve them with meal planning.** Have them plan a night's dinner, take them shopping, have them help you read through cookbooks, or buy them their own. The more involved they are, the more excited they will be about participating at dinnertime, from eating to talking to loading the dishwasher.

✔ **Set up a family menu.** Place a piece of paper on the refrigerator listing what every meal will be that week. Leave flexibility for ordering out, or eating on the

©ISTOCKPHOTO.COM/DIGITAL SKILLET

go. Remind everyone of the meal planned for the next day so they are prepared and can't complain when dinner is served.

✔ **Try small portions of veggies, and work your way up.** Veggies are always the big battle. As babies, youngsters eat almost every kind of veggie smashed and watered down but stop eating them as they get older. Even if they won't eat them, put a couple on their plate. Seeing them there will keep it in their minds that they need to eat it for a balanced diet.

✔ **Give gentle praise for good eating, but don't overdo it.** You don't want to use food as emotional blackmail.

✔ **Be realistic/flexible.** You know your child. Be accommodating. . . to a point. Remember, you have your freezer and your

Make Peace With Your Own Food Issues

Don't bring your own issues with food to the table. Parents who diet constantly or make negative comments about their bodies or certain foods in front of their children, no matter how young, can pass along those same distortions to their children.

Don't force the issue of veggies and fruits, but do try to include small portions at every meal.

pre-prepared and packaged foods, so if one kid wants meatloaf one night, and another wants chicken, it doesn't have to be a big deal.

✔ **Don't make them clean their plate.** Children's appetites vary. Just like you. They may be starving one night, hardly eat the next. Don't stress out about it. Instead, remind them of the benefits of healthy eating. By now they are learning about how their bodies grow. If they want to build muscles, have healthy hair, and want to be as big as mommy and daddy, they need to eat nutritiously.

✔ **Cut out unhealthy snacks.** Stock nutritious items like fruit, whole grain bread, cereals, and crackers in the house. That includes eliminating sugary drinks, which fill kids up.

✔ **Sneak it in.** Mix beans into spaghetti sauce meat dishes, or blueberries into brownies. I'm also big on adding fruits, like peaches, oranges, watermelon, and apples to salads for variety and more nutrients.

✔ **Pick your battles.** If they don't want to eat what you're serving, they don't eat. Or they can get up and make themselves a peanut butter sandwich. The bigger deal you make out of them not eating, the more likely they are going to respond by rejecting the foods you offer.

By packing healthy lunches, you encourage healthy eating.

Dishing at the Dinner Table

The trick is to avoid the mundane (How am I getting to tennis? Who's driving me to piano?) and get your kids engaged. Some ideas:

- Bring a map of the U.S. or a globe of the world. Have someone pick a place—just close your eyes and point—and then ask various family members what they know about that area. If no one knows the answers, make that a project for the next night's conversation.

- If you have tweens and teens: Listen to their music, watch their TV shows, read their school-required books, so you can discuss something from their world.

- Have a "talk-about-it bowl:" Family members can put items in a large container that you place in the middle of the table, maybe a flower, an article from a maga-zine, a school paper, possibly even a recipe someone wants Mom or Dad to try. This forms the basis for a conversation that evening.

- Respect when a child doesn't want to talk, but remind her she still has to sit at the table.

Offer healthy snacks, but stop by 4:30 p.m. so they will want to eat dinner.

✔ **Make dinner fun.** Add theme nights to your meal planner. Kids look forward to taco night or breakfast for dinner.

✔ **Encourage them to invite friends over.** Kids are more willing to try the foods their friends eat, and also tend to talk more at dinnertime.

✔ **Don't make food the focus.** Yes, you want to establish healthy eating habits, but don't make food a big-deal topic. If you're constantly counting calories or worrying about your body shape, kids will pick up on it. Likewise, using food as rewards or bribes just makes it into more of an issue.

✔ **Respect eating quirks.** Kids may avoid the crust on their sandwich or the tips of a hot dog. Children are allowed to be picky and fussy. What they eat today might not be eaten tomorrow. Ultimately, it is their decision what they want to eat. No doubt, they will make up the nutrition later in the day or later that week. Let it go.

Tweens and Teens

✔ **Keep hunger at bay with a pantry full of healthy snacks** such as carrots and hummus, crackers and salami.

✔ **Make dinner in a crock pot.** This way busy teens know there is a hot meal ready. They can help with the preparation by making a salad.

✔ **Avoid power struggles over food.** Teens are looking for reasons to pick a fight with you and exert their independence, so responding by commenting on their over- or under-eating will just set off fireworks.

✔ **Involve your kids with menu planning.** This is something you should be doing through the ages and doesn't change as your kids get older. In fact, they should be more involved.

✔ **Use texting to your advantage.** Ask them via text what they might want this week. Or send them messages from the kitchen with a time-for-dinner countdown (five more minutes!) so they know there is no excuse for not sitting down together with the family.

✔ **Keep a pizza or taco night,** or whatever your teenager likes on your meal planning rotation as a way to get them excited about dinner. Make it healthy by adding a salad or putting veggies and protein on pizza.

Be Alert to Signs of Eating Disorders

Adolescence is often when kids feel pressure to limit what they eat so they can obtain a certain look. If your son or daughter habitually refuses to eat, is losing weight, is secretive about eating, and disappears to the bathroom after meals, it could be a sign of an eating disorder. Talk to your child's doctor before this becomes an issue.

✔ **Encourage them to invite friends over.** Teens talk more with friends at the table, and this helps to set up the ritual of family meals as enjoyable and memorable times.

✔ **Add calcium** (critical to bone development). Teens require the calcium equivalent of about four 8-ounce glasses of milk daily. Look for items that are rich in Vitamin D, like cheeses and yogurts.

✔ **Stock up on protein and iron.** Busy teens often choose processed and convenience foods over fresh. This is the time of growth and development, meaning developing teens need lots of calories and good nutrients. Good choices of iron-rich foods include beef, chicken, pork, eggs, spinach, green peas, beans, nuts, rice, and pasta.

✔ **Cut out junk foods and soda and encourage breakfast.** Make sure to include some kind of protein for continued energy as a breakfast starter. Ideally, breakfast should include fruit or fruit juice, toast, eggs. Place articles from websites and magazines in a place where they will see them, so they can read for themselves. At this age, learning from a third party is always better than hearing it from Mom.

Encourage breakfast: All kids need an energy boast. Don't forget YOU!

Easy Snacks for Tweens/Teens

- Cut up celery and place it in an inch of water in a jar in the refrigerator. Encourage teens to spread peanut butter or cream cheese on top for added taste.

- Crackers with sliced cheese and salami also make great snacks; again peanut butter and cream cheese are good additions.

- Have baby carrots on hand with hummus dip or ranch dressing.

- Stock fruit as easy grab-and-go foods, i.e., bananas, apples, pears, and peaches.

- Have a blender on the counter for easy fruit and yogurt smoothies.

- Make your own trail or party mix. Combine nuts, dried fruit, and favorite cereals, and store in a Tupperware container.

- Stock hard boiled eggs in the fridge.

- Make it easy for them to make sandwiches with plenty of bread, bagels, and cold cuts. Or be creative and encourage a waffle sandwich—two whole grain toasted waffles with peanut butter or cheese.

Athletic teens need extra calories, iron-rich foods, and fluids.

✔ **Teach them about "smart fats."** This is the time when adolescents often restrict their fat intake in order to stay trim. When they cut out fat in general, they also cut out healthy fats. Remind your kids, especially girls striving to look like models in *Seventeen Magazine*, that healthful eating is a challenge for everyone, even for those who make it look easy. They may not be willing to talk face to face about this but, if you can, chat via texting about proper food choices.

✔ **Remind them to eat and drink right.** Teens, primarily those on-the-go athletic types, need extra calories (as much as 4,000 a day), as they burn them quickly. If your teen is involved in sports, encourage him to choose more iron-containing foods, such as meat, vegetables, and grains. He also should be drinking a bevy of extra fluids to prevent dehydration. Make sure your teen carries a water bottle at all times.

Dealing with Picky Eaters

Most kids, especially toddlers, will go through a picky-eater stage. It's normal, and in fact, *expected*. Accept that children are changing and will go through phases. Most often, it's not about food at all, but about wanting control of a situation. Children learn from a very young age how to get a rise out of you (often when they reject food, and you plead with them to eat it). The more response you give, the more, or less, behavior you will get from your child. Do your best not to overreact.

* **Be realistic.** Toddlers usually don't reject the food you've prepared for them in order to drive you crazy. At this age, a child's appetite can temporarily wane when teething or if they're tired. One tactic: Try new foods earlier in the day when your toddler has more energy.

* **Consider the source.** Beth Oden, a mom of two and a Boulder, Colorado-based family nutrition coach who works with parents, says there's a difference between a picky eater and a "food fighter." The picky eater truly has some taste issues determined around texture, color, or smell, meaning it could be something about the sensation with the food that's truly a bother. The "food fighter" on the other hand, is the child who is going through a developmental stage (usually around age two) and trying to establish his independence and gain some control. You know your child best. Determine which one is your child, and go from there.

* **Serve a variety of healthy foods every day with no pressure.** Avoid pleading and cajoling kids to eat. As long as you serve a variety of healthy foods every day, your toddler will find something on his plate to eat.

* **Don't use dessert as leverage.** We've all done it: We've used the dreaded words, "If you don't eat all your dinner you won't get dessert." But

Did you know?

Cooking together strengthens feelings of responsibility, and being a valued member of the team helps to form a lifetime of good memories and helps to strengthen bonds.

Mom Tip

"Once my kids hit 6th grade, they had to take turns cooking and planning meals. I'd go grocery shopping on Sunday afternoons, and, before I left the house, I'd have a sit-down with each child as to what breakfast and lunch preferences they had and what meals they would like for that week. This way, my kids quickly learned that there was no complaining, and I was not a short-order cook."

—Maureen Doolan Boyle, East Islip, NY, mom of six, ages 17 to 24

what we've really said here (without knowing it) is that dessert is the best food ever, and what they're having for dinner is awful. Do not use dessert as leverage, just as you shouldn't use big rewards as leverage either. Small rewards, such as stickers, an extra book at bedtime, ten more minutes of computer time, is OK. Be reasonable.

* **Get kids involved.** This has been a big mantra of mine so far. But if you make grocery shopping and cooking fun, your picky eater is more apt to try new foods.

* **Be a positive role model.** Children, even young toddlers, are highly suggestible. If you'd like your child to eat broccoli, then you should, too.

* **Praise each and every nibble.** Congratulate them for tasting and trying. To encourage more bites, ask them questions about what it tasted like. Gently ask them to take a few more bites, maybe with ketchup or salt?

* **Keep trying.** Although some toddlers may readily gobble up any food you put in front of them, many will not. Research suggests it may take ten or more exposures to new foods before children accept them.

* **Sign a food treaty.** Heather Schoenrock of Duluth, Georgia, admits she has a couple of picky eaters and didn't like that her dinner table was becoming a war zone. As a way to restore peace at the table, she and her five-year-old came up with a list of the "Unarguable 12," 12 food items that her daughter, Sadie, will *not* argue about with

her if served. Sadie was required to choose two veggies and two fruits, and the rest was pretty much free of mom's interference. "On the list was mac and cheese—no surprise there—chicken, rice, broccoli, green beans, grapes, apples, and a few other healthy and not-so-healthy choices. Key here is that they were her choices," says Heather. "She then signed this food treaty, and we posted it on the fridge. It makes me a very happy mom to be able to point to this list and nip a potential blow-up in the bud."

* **Relax.** If your child doesn't have a medical issue, is moving along on the growth chart, if thriving and gaining weight, then relax. It's not horrible for a tantruming child to go to bed without dinner one night. It's often more a guilt problem for you. Think of it like weaning your baby off the bottle, stresses nutrition coach Beth. Let them cry it out. Let them go to bed hungry. Yes, you'll have to deal with the inconvenience (i.e., a tired, tantruming kid), but if you buckle and give in to tantrums over food, guess who has the power?

Kids in the Kitchen

When my girls were little, we played "let's make a concoction." I'd give them a plastic bowl (I usually set it in on the floor or at their kiddie table.) and then have them pick out items from the fridge and cabinets, e.g., flour, sugar, ketchup, mustard, whipped

Use plastic measuring cups, bowls, and baking dishes, as they are safer for kids.

Expert Advice: Ellyn Satter Tips
Your Child Will Grow Up To Get the Right Body

Your child has a natural way of growing that is right for her, and she knows how much she needs to eat to grow that way. Her inborn way of growing is supported by, and in balance with, her inborn tendency to consume more or less food and her inborn tendency to be more or less active. If you maintain a division of responsibility in feeding and a division of responsibility in activity, including trusting her to do her part with eating and moving, you don't need to worry about her growing normally—it will happen.

Your child's body shape and size are mostly inherited. He will resemble you with respect to being big, small, or in-between. His height and weight are normal for him as long as he grows consistently, even if his growth plots at the extreme upper or lower ends of the growth charts—above the 97th or below the 3rd percentiles. But if

his weight or height abruptly and rapidly shift up or down on his growth chart, it can indicate a problem. In that case, consult a health professional who understands feeding dynamics, to rule out health, feeding, or parenting problems.

Children who are unusual in any way—in this instance, those who are especially big or small—need particularly good social skills. Rather than trying to change your child's size or shape, which will backfire, concentrate on teaching your child to cope. Help her to develop good character, common sense, effective ways of responding to feelings, problem-solving skills, and the ability to get along with others.

To help your child grow in the way that is right for him or her:

● Feed in the best way. Follow the division of responsibility in feeding.

● Limit television, and give your child opportunities to be active. Follow the division of responsibility in activity.

● Feel good about the body your child has, not the one you thought she would have.

Let children assist you. Kids will try anything if they can help cook it.

cream, etc., and let them mix them all together and, yes, get messy (part of the fun). I'd encourage them to use spices so they could get a sense for different aromas, and even put a tiny taste on their mouth. Certainly what they were stirring was never something we ate, but had I been more organized, it could have been.

At the time I wasn't thinking about anything other than giving them an activity in the kitchen, where I could keep an eye on them and still cook dinner. But in hindsight, I realize this was a pretty good tactic for getting them to enjoy the cooking process. Seeing me stir and add and have them be enveloped in the robust aromas of whatever I was cooking, even if it was just hot dogs (I love the smell of boiled hot dogs.), was a way to get them involved in the process and instill some joy into the kitchen experience.

You might not want to think about it when

Dinner Made Easy

What's the next best thing to a fairy godmother who brings dinner to your family's table? My new savior: HealtyPantry.com, nutritious meals in a box. (You just add the meat.)

Designed by a dad of three (and how can we not love men who cook?), these recipe kits make cooking and eating at home easy as pie. . . or easy as skillet lasagna, turkey stew, wild salmon patties, or whatever you choose. (They even have low-sugar, vegetarian and gluten-free kits).

Get your teens interested in cooking by letting them bake chocolate chip cookies. Those, coupled with a glass of milk, are healthier than store-bought snacks.

Mom Tip

"Mix your own favorite spice blend—if you cook with the same types of spices repeatedly, pre-mix a batch and put it in its own jar so you cut time pulling a half-dozen jars out of the pantry when you cook."

—Julie Parrish West Linn, OR, mom of three, ages 6, 8,. and 9

your baby is an adorable cooing infant or even a defiant toddler, but the truth is, it's our job as parents to empower our children to eventually go out into the world and live on their own. With that means learning responsibility for cooking (and even laundry—another book). The earlier you can involve your kids in the kitchen, the better. They don't have to cook per say, but they can certainly help.

Aside from being a tasty (and messy) experience, it's also great for helping little ones develop motor skills. Plus it introduces them to new vocabulary and math concepts, as they see you reading food labels and recipes and using measuring cups. You can also involve them, based on their age, in multiplying and dividing when you need to figure out how to half or double a recipe.

As for when you can let kids cook or prep in the kitchen without supervision, that's up to you. Certainly when kids are young (and if you place things in safe low cabinets), they can learn to pour their own cereal or grab snacks out of the pantry. I'm a big believer in advocating that they learn to help themselves to milk and juice too. At six or seven, with supervision, they can even use the blender to make smoothies.

In general, children under 12 should be supervised at all times, especially around anything hot or sharp. But even then, a 14- or 16-year-old can mess up. You know your child best. My family still likes to talk about the time my then-14-year-old used the teapot to boil miso soup. (There went the teapot.) She remains a bit of a klutz in the kitchen, while my younger one is cautious and disciplined. Whatever you do, just be sure you always explain the risks and dangers of a kitchen, and make sure your kids understand the rules for what they are and aren't allowed to do in the kitchen without you.

Some basic strategies for getting youngsters involved in the kitchen:

✔ **Act excited about cooking and baking.** If you show your kids that you enjoy cooking, they'll want to be right there with you chopping, mixing, and baking.

✔ **Let them help.** That can be anything from washing and tearing lettuce, gathering

Inspire Your Young Cook

Books are great ways to motivate your kids to help you in the kitchen. Some of my favorites:

Bean Appetit: Hip and Healthy Ways to Have Fun with Food (hardcover), by Shannon Payette Seip and Kelly Parthen

FamilyFun: Cooking with Kids, by Deanna F. Cook

Cooking Fun: 121 Simple Recipes to Make with Kids (hardcover), by Rae Grant

Kids Cooking: A Very Slightly Messy Manual, by the editors of Klutz

Salad People and More Real Recipes: A New Cookbook for Preschoolers and Up, by Mollie Katzen

C is for Cooking: Recipes from the Street (Sesame Street!), by Susan McQuillan, M.S., R.D.

The Sleep Over Cookbook, by Hallie Warshaw

See more resources at the end of this book.

Note to Self

You control what, where and when food is provided.

Your child decides how much and whether or not to eat the food.

Mom Tip

"I absolutely do not allow my boys to eat any veggies or fruits. Things like spinach, broccoli, watermelon, corn, etc., all give kids 'superhero powers' and build 'really big muscles.' I usually start with none of these things on their plate. A bunch goes on my plate and dad's, and we make it a game—'Max, your muscles are already waaaay too big. No, you can't have more than a small bite!' Then we all laugh as they end up eating tons of veggies. My five-year-old (who pretty much gets it now) still loves this game."

—Cindy Parker, Laguna Beach, CA, mom of two, ages 5 and 3

items from your pantry, writing down lists of needed grocery items, or stirring batter.

✔ **Take them food shopping.** Explain why you choose one item over another (less sodium and salt). Make it a fun game to search for the right crackers, snacks, etc.

✔ **Encourage their input with meal planning.** Pick a day that's theirs, meaning they get to select the entrée and the dessert. Give them ownership, as well as some ground rules (i.e., some protein, veggies, starch, etc.). The more responsibility you give them the better—and the better the odds that they'll try something new and be proud of what they make. Kelly Parthen, co-author of *Bean Appetit: Hip and Healthy Ways to Have Fun with Food,* and mom of two, goes one step further by challenging kids to come up with a meal that is all the same color (e.g., a "green gobbler" meal). It's also fun for them to come up with meal/food names. Baked chicken becomes "dinosaur bones" at her table.

✔ **Make it manageable.** Buy easy-to-prep items, or pre-prep so it's easier to involve them in the cooking process. Where you can, be as hands-off as possible, and allow them to experiment (and yes, make messes and mistakes). It's all part of the learning process.

✔ **Let them make mistakes.** By adding too much salt or sugar to a recipe they'll become better at reading recipes.

✔ **Challenge them as they grow,** by asking them to help you with more creative

Make food shopping fun by treating it like a scavenger hunt.

menus (some international cuisine, perhaps?) and giving them more responsibility.

✔ **Make the meals interactive.** Again, an idea from Colorado Springs, Colorado, mom Kelly who says, "Rather than serving tacos, do taco towers instead. Serve all the ingredients, with chips instead of shells, and see who can make, and eat, the tallest tower." She packs "cracker stackers" for her little one's lunch often—a great way to encourage healthy eating.

✔ **Grow a vegetable garden.** There's something to be said about eating foods the child planted. When my daughter, Sydney, planted a tomato plant in a pa-

fyi

Looking for a cost-effective way to learn what's best to feed your kids and how? Check out the nutritional DVD series "Max's Minutes—The A-Zs of Healthy Living" MaxsMinutes.com by Denver-based nutritionist Julie Hammerstein. Or go to MaxLifeTherapies.com.

Plant A Garden With Your Child

Kids tend to be more interested in eating what they have helped to grow. Start small. Think about how much space you have and the age of your child. Also think about your time: The last thing you need is to be overwhelmed with another task, not to mention weeds. Miniature vegetable varieties by your windowsill are more accessible and understandable to small children. Ask at your local gardening center for what works best for your lifestyle (small space vs. large space,  amount of light, etc.). You should also ask about what kind of veggies do well in small containers so your child can really take ownership.

Remember, though, to purchase disease- and pest-resistant plants. Children love to touch, and fingers often end up in their mouths, so organic and pesticide-free plants are safest. Vegetables that are fairly problem-free include beets, carrots, cucumbers, onions, peas, radishes, spinach, and rhubarb.

per cup in her first grade classroom, she was more apt to eat it once it grew.

✔ **Embrace the mess.** It's bound to happen.

✔ **Be patient.** It can be a hassle with little ones in the kitchen, but taking the time to train them early helps them (and more important, you) as they get older.

Easy Jobs Even Little Kids Can Do

Giving your kids chores from a young age teaches them responsibility and accountability, plus it shows them the work, and teamwork, it takes to run a household. Put on some music and make it fun. Or set a timer and see who can get all their chores done before it goes off.

✱ Put silverware away. Set a stool or chair by the silverware drawer, and watch their pride when they put each item in the right section. (No knives though.)

* Sweep the floors, put things in the trash, load and unload the dishwasher, and wipe the table. Clean up is as important as set up.

* Set the table.

* Put leftovers in a container and then store in the fridge.

* Bring you the items you need while cooking.

Feeding Vegetarian Kids

The good news: Your child announces he or she wants to be a vegetarian (or maybe already is one because you're one). This is a great opening to educate your child and the rest of your family about nutrition, good food choices, and

All kids love pasta. Take some beans and veggies, mash or puree them and add to sauce—kids will never know.

fyi

It doesn't take a rocket scientist to know that the hardest part of planning any meal is figuring out what to have. Go to theFoodNanny.com where food guru Liz Edmunds offers "theme nights," along with other recipes and meal plans. A lifesaver.

Stock up on proteins for your vegetarian child.

Mom Tip

"I've always made baby food by adding interesting flavors like basil or mint. and she always ate enthusiastically. I also create fun combinations like sweet potatoes and cinnamon, apples and plums, chicken and mushrooms, etc. My 15-month-old now loves things like salmon, baba ghanoush, and my homemade soups."

—Maureen Smithe Brusznicki, Chicago, IL, mom of two, an infant and a 15-month-old, HomemadeMothering.com

creative new ways to eat well.

The bad news: If you're not a vegetarian, and your child just decided to become one, you need to switch gears to accommodate his or her new tastes.

For the sake of brevity and simplicity, I'm going to assume you're a meat eater but your kid isn't. If you're already a vegetarian, you *know* what to serve your child and what to shop for—after all, you've already been doing it for *you*. But if this is suddenly thrust on you, like it is for many parents when their kids reach tween-hood, you might be a bit more stuck on what to serve for dinner (and breakfast and lunch).

Being a vegetarian also means different things to different people. For some, it's a complete elimination of any kind of meat, including seafood. In general, most kids who define themselves as vegetarians fall into the ovo-lacto (egg and dairy products) category, meaning that they eat eggs and dairy products. Ovo-vegetarians eat eggs but not dairy. Lacto-vegetarians are the exact opposite, consuming dairy but not eggs. Vegans consume no animal products whatsoever. In common usage, the word vegetarian encompasses all these categories, though vegans sometimes choose to differentiate themselves.

Some decide to go vegetarian because their friends are doing it (like my friend Lynn's daughter Lauren did at age 10), or others because of the cruelty-to-animals issue (like my friend Elisha's daughter Sophie did at 12). For some it's a phase, for others a lifelong passion.

Your job as Mom is to make sure you're offering enough variety to please everyone at the table, or as Lynn says, "ensure everyone is not eating pasta all the time."

The bottom line: One cannot simply eliminate an entire food group without replacing it with good quality and variety of vegetarian alternatives. And so, when your child makes a decision on the kind of vegetarian he or she is, you'll need to stock up on foods that meet his or her criteria.

For my college roommate Lynn, whose daughter, Lauren, decided in fifth grade that she wanted to be a vegetarian, it meant eating no meat, but including fish and eggs. For my friend Elisha, whose daughter, Sophie, won't eat fish but will eat dairy, it means strategizing what's for dinner without alienating the other members of the family.

Which means stocking up on lots of proteins, such as whole grains, soy products, beans, and nuts. Lynn is big on keeping her freezer filled with bean burritos and frozen vegetarian soups and chilis. Elisha likes

Refresh With Water

I'll admit to storing potato chips and crackers in our house, which aren't so healthy, but what I'm really strict about is what I serve my kids to drink. The mainstay drink in our house is water. We avoid soda at all costs. Why? It fills kids up with either empty calories or artificial sweeteners, and often contains caffeine. It's also bad to have acidic, sugary liquid passing over your child's teeth and gums all day long. It also fills them up so they're less apt to eat their dinner. If your family likes these drinks, save them for an occasional, special treat.

Mom Tip

"I have two young children who hardly eat anything besides mac and cheese and chicken nuggets and won't leave me in the kitchen for an hour to prepare a culinary delight. As a result, I've learned to streamline it. I buy a lot of prepared foods at Whole Foods. I also make double on-the-side dishes so we have plenty of choices."

—Shane Okoon Shaps,
Louisville, KY, mom of
two, ages 3 and 5

creating meals that do double-duty, like spaghetti sauce that can be made with or without meat. "I try to do things that have the same base, and then add the meat portions later for my husband and me," she says.

Both have grown to accommodate their daughters' choices and admit their families have gotten more health-conscious as a result of eating less red meat and more fish.

They are also adamant about keeping up with pediatrician visits to make sure their girls are getting enough calcium and iron and are growing and gaining weight appropriately.

Experts advise watching out for vegetarian kids gorging on junk food like potato chips and pizza. After all, they're still kids and not always going to make the best choices. Some suggest putting the onus on your child. If he or she made this decision, then he or she should be more responsible for letting you know what they want when it's time to write up your meal plans or grocery lists. As long as your child is eating a wide variety of foods, especially grains and beans for protein, and as long as he/she is growing and getting the OK from their doc, there's no need to worry. All it takes on your part is helping them to make good food choices and going from "what we cannot eat" to "what we choose to eat." As Elisha says, "It's really not that hard."

The Allergic Child

There are so many allergies out there today, from minor to severe, that you need to be careful when cooking/catering to the allergic child. (Make sure to always ask when inviting friends of your kids over for dinner.) All of which makes the dilemma of what to serve either for yourselves or your guests more challenging.

Needless to say, parents of children with allergies need to be more adept at reading food

> ### Mom Tip
>
> *"Bone health is crucial for growing teens. I made sure my kids got at least one of each of the Big Three (milk, yogurt, cheese) every day. It's key to make sure that your kid is getting enough calcium and vitamin D. I also always had packets of string cheese and individual packs of cheese. Milk was a staple as was orange juice with calcium. I also got yogurts in practically every form. Go-gurts® were the best."*
>
> —Katerina Canyon,
> Marina del Rey, CA, mom of two,
> ages 17 and 21

Peanuts are increasingly a big no-no.

Fewer than 10% of U.S. high school students are eating the combined recommended daily amount of fruits and vegetables, according to the Centers for Disease Control and Prevention.

labels and avoiding certain foods in their house. It could be as simple as creating a separate shelf for "Jake's foods" or completely eliminating anything with peanut oil from your shelves. The good news: Many stores offer well-stocked health food sections offering chemical- and additive-free meats, poultry, and fish, along with other items, most of which are healthier for the entire family.

The key is to cater to your allergic child without alienating other family members, and making sure you're not stressing by making ten meals every night.

The truth is, there are a lot of food choices out there today, with shortcuts, recipes and frozen entrees that cater to peanut-free, gluten-free, and lactose-intolerant sensitivities. You're sure to find a recipe out there where, as with the vegetarian child, you can use one base and then substitute, or throw in other proteins to accommodate everyone's likes and dislikes. Since we're all about "teachable moments," use this one to educate your kids about healthy alternatives and choices. Some resources: *Feeding Your Allergic Child* by Elisa Meyer and *The Allergy Free Cookbook* by Eileen Ruhude Yoder. Also see aNutritionMission.com, the website run by mom Beth Oden, who has two allergic children and a degree in nutrition.

6

Feed Yourself First

We moms are a judgmental lot. The stay-at-homes vs. the work-outside-the-homes. The organic vs. the non-organic. The PTA-involved vs. the non-PTA-involved. And, yes, even the "We eat dinner together five nights a week and that includes a home cooked meal," vs. the often too-embarrassed to admit, "We do take-out five nights a week, rarely see each other, let alone eat together, and always have the TV on in the background."

Many wear our *momness* like a badge of honor with one-upmanship here, there, and everywhere: Little Jake who walked and talked at ten months, Sarah whose ballet prowess is the talk of the neighborhood, Max the star athlete, and Carly who whizzed through her SATs. We stand behind them (or in front of them) often claiming their victory as our own. After all, it's we who tutored them, drove them, coached them, catered to them, pampered them, and fed them.

No matter what path we choose, there's always some level of guilt involved that we did

Use the computer as a tool to help your kids shop with you—or help you select which Chinese dish to order. The bottom line: You spending time together.

Mom Tip

"I strongly believe in raising your children as part of your household and teaching them responsibility. My kids started helping to set the table before they were two years old. Now at four, my daughter carries the drinks to the table and helps clean it up. They even dump their leftovers in the garbage and put their stuff in the dishwasher."

—Peg Mischler, Neenah, WI, mom of two, ages 2 and 4

or didn't do the *right* things, including doing too much or too little. Either we're perceived as society's little darling who can do it all because we actually have time to shop and cook and rein in our families for nightly meals; or we feel shame for not being able to provide that rosy Norman Rockwell suburban family experience, and so think we're shortchanging our families in some way.

What is it about us women that makes it so difficult for us to simply be content with what we can do and resigned to what we can't? And since when did the yardstick for our parenting skills boil down to the family meal?

We all know the statistics about how healthy family meals are for everyone and, in particular, how this ritual cuts down on teenage substance abuse. And we all know that they nourish us in more ways than one, by having us connect at the end of a long day, comforting us with warm dishes of casseroles and stews.

There are some appropriate sayings. Perhaps you've heard them. *Strength in numbers. Girl power. It takes a village.*

We need to lean on each other more. Be honest with each other. Be honest with ourselves. Stop trying to be the "perfect mom" and be happy with "good enough."

We also need to stick to that other famous saying: *Feed your soul.*

In other words, ladies, it's hard to feed others when you're not feeding yourselves. Granted, I'm using feeding both metaphorically and figuratively, but you know what I mean. It doesn't take a rocket scientist to know we moms are stressed. And it doesn't matter if we're single, married, in the corporate world, or at home with our kids. We're tired. Overworked. Overstretched. Often

Mom Tip

"Find some simple, quick recipes that include a protein, complex carbohydrate, and vegetable, and that most of your family likes. You can never please everyone, so don't try."

—Shannah Godfrey, Independence, MO, mom of 14, grandmother to 11

"Be accommodating—to a degree. I give my kids the option of our family dinner, or a cheese sandwich. The caveat is that they have to have a bite of everything the adults eat."

—Amanda Louden, Gold River, CA, mom of two, ages 5 and 7

There's nothing wrong with ordering in…and inviting friends over is even better.

Things for Dinner You Might Not Have Thought Of

A frittata. Toss in leftover veggies.

Stuffed baked potatoes. Throw in cheese, broccoli, chili, and it's a meal.

Soup (add salad and bread, and you have a hearty dinner).

Sandwiches. Mix it up by using foccacia bread instead of regular slices, or grill up paninis (no panini pan required!).

French toast. Add fruit on top.

running, running, running, until our gauge is near empty. Why use that energy to try and one-up each other instead of just being content with the best we can do.

We need to stop beating ourselves up. Sure, there are some things we could do better. And yes it's important to try and fix what's not working. But at your core, you should know you're not ruining your kids for life if you don't sit down for a family meal seven nights a week. Nor are you setting your kids up for failure if that meal isn't home cooked, and set on a perfectly clutter-free table. The bottom line: You need to energize yourself in order to fuel your family. We moms need to be more honest with ourselves—and others—that we can't do it all without some compromises.

It's simple really. Just like they say before take-off on an airplane, put your oxygen mask on first, and then deal with your little ones. In other words: Do for you first so you *can* take care of your family. And if that means someone else picks up dinner, or batch cooking on a Sunday, or bringing in prepared foods nine times out of ten, then so be it.

Yes, this book is about the importance of family meals. But it's about accepting your schedules and limitations. Granted, you're most likely reading this because you know you can do better. But we can all do better. There's no magic number for success. Success is defined by your family. And by you.

Yes, you can be more organized. And yes, you can strategize ways to get everyone together more often, but remember that this is a process that doesn't happen overnight. There is no "gold standard" other than the one you set for yourself. Whatever it takes to make it

Creamy Coffee Wake-Up Call

Ingredients

- ❑ ¼ cup lowfat milk
- ❑ ½ to 1 teaspoon instant coffee
- ❑ 4 lowfat or fat free milk ice cubes cracked
- ❑ ½ banana, sliced
- ❑ 2 tablespoons brown sugar or chocolate syrup
- ❑ ¼ teaspoon vanilla extract
- ❑ Ground cinnamon or chocolate (optional)

Power sipping!

I'm a coffee fanatic, which is why I love this easy (healthy) pick me up.

Make milk ice cubes (fill an ice cube tray with milk, about 1 to 1 ½ cups for the whole tray; freeze 3 hours or until solid). To crack cubes, crush with mallet or rolling pin; store extra cubes in a plastic zipper bag.

Combine milk, instant coffee, milk ice cubes, banana, brown sugar, and vanilla in an electric blender. Whirl until smooth. Sprinkle with ground cinnamon or chocolate if desired.

Play With Your Food—Or At Least Wear It

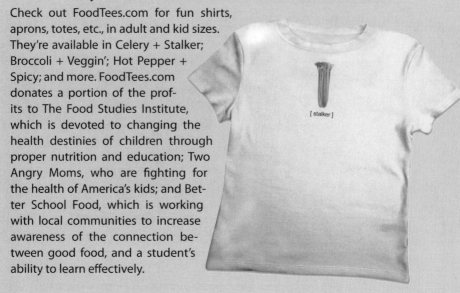

Check out FoodTees.com for fun shirts, aprons, totes, etc., in adult and kid sizes. They're available in Celery + Stalker; Broccoli + Veggin'; Hot Pepper + Spicy; and more. FoodTees.com donates a portion of the profits to The Food Studies Institute, which is devoted to changing the health destinies of children through proper nutrition and education; Two Angry Moms, who are fighting for the health of America's kids; and Better School Food, which is working with local communities to increase awareness of the connection between good food, and a student's ability to learn effectively.

[stalker]

work is whatever it takes. So, stop feeling guilty. And stop making the mom next-door feel guilty. If you're the one with time on your hands, in fact, do her a favor, and make an extra meatloaf for her family one of these days. Cooking for others has always helped in lifting my soul. (And I like receiving too, so send me your recipes and tips!)

Block Out Me Time

I bet you often feel as I do—Like my body is a vending machine, constantly dispensing money, offering advice, helping with homework, dealing with deadlines, and always providing, giving, doing, driving, errand-running, multi-tasking. There are days when I'm literally drained. Depleted. Zonked. But with all my responsibilities and obligations, it's not possible to close down for a day or two and sleep it off. Which is why I try (key word: Try) to eliminate my energy drains so I can recharge.

I know you're with me, girlfriend. Our mom settings seem to be ON and OFF with no in between. And often that OFF switch doesn't occur until 10 p.m., when we literally crash. Therapeutic lifestyle educator Taiha Wagner of Eden Prairie, Minnesota (JustOneBite.net), says we moms set a high standard for ourselves that is often unrealistic. In our guts we want to create a home-cooked meal with everyone around the table, but it's not always possible, so we beat ourselves up about what we're not doing, as opposed to all the good we *are* doing. She has moms that pay her to do meal planning and grocery lists, just so they can get more organized and put their families on healthier paths. "Most moms who haven't tried the 20 or 30 minutes it takes to plan a week's worth of menus or shopping lists really do not understand the power they have in reducing their stress and anxiety throughout the week," says the mom of three.

Taiha also is big on having moms keep an activity log so they can see where their energy drains are. This includes how much sleep they're getting, what they're eating, and when and how much down time they have. Once these moms see in black and white how crazy their days are, the lack of fun they're having, how poorly they're eating, and the junk they're putting in their bodies, they are able to change their routines and lose some of the guilt. She encourages them to put more music into their day, to plan for down time, and to make their lives simpler. Easier said than done? Again, it's a process, but once you commit to figuring out your time and energy drains, it all—including what's for dinner—becomes a lot easier.

✔ **First, look at what's consuming you.** Is it overcommiting? Work? Aging parents? Spousal demands? Your kids? Lack of community? Debt? Clutter? Envy? And then deal with them. Start saying no to things you can't do. When you say no to others, you say yes to yourself (and your family).

Tip

Hard boil a few eggs once a week, then refrigerate them. That way you always have some quick protein on hand—for a salad, a to-go breakfast, or a sliced-up snack.

Mom Tip

"*I think many families feel pressured to get it right all the time, which is unrealistic and will only lead to a sense of failure. It's important for families to give themselves permission to be imperfect sometimes.*"

—Liz Sawyer Danowski , Oxford, England, mom of one son, age 5

Tools of the Trade

Invest in the right appliances:

A crock pot

A toaster oven

Good knives

A hand blender

Lasagna pan

Heavy-gauge, stainless steel
six-quart sauté pan

Sauce pans

George Forman indoor grill

For more serious cooks: A Cuisinart

Mom Tip

"In general, the rule is that we eat together as a family, no TV. We talk and interact at dinner, which I think helps keep my son interested in staying at the table for more than five minutes. I also try to make his food fun. I recently made polenta cut into star shapes that he really enjoyed. I also think dips are key. They keep the child engaged and you can sneak in a lot of nutrition... anything from cheese sauce with hidden squash puree, to a thinned-out white bean dip."

—Shannon Paterson, Boise,
ID, mom of one, age 3

✔ **Schedule time for YOU.** Pencil in at least five minutes every day for yourself to just relax and do whatever you feel like doing. Obviously, more time is better, but all it takes to retain emotional health is to get a break from your everyday chaotic work schedule. Remember to punch that little break into your timecard just like corporate America gets. If you work at home, allow yourself ON and OFF time.

✔ **The truth is: My mom taught me to be selfish.** She always had a life of her own—a job she enjoyed, a group of tennis gals she played with on Sunday mornings, an alfresco walk alone around the block after dinner as a way to clear her head. It never bothered me that she was missing for an hour or two. In fact, I guess I subconsciously learned from a young age that I needed time for me too.

It's a trait many women aren't taught. My friend, Elisha recently told me how she envied the fact that I always make time for myself. "It's not something I schedule or think to do," she said. Which really struck me because I sort of *have* to have some time for me, or I turn into this Jekyll-and-Hyde personality who's super moody, impatient, and an all-around crank. In other words, it's ugly. And not something I'm proud of. But I'm fanatical about needing time for myself in order to function. Sometimes it's a quick five minutes lying on my bed with an herbal pillow, or sitting in my favorite chair in our living room with *People Magazine* (my guilty pleasure). But it's five minutes for me, and my family has learned to let me have my moment.

✓ **Don't clean as much.** My house is a mess, and I don't care. OK, I care a little… but I've decided I'd rather have peace of mind over eliminating the dust bunnies. That means the occasional dirty dishes in the sink or the pile of laundry that sits there while I do something more meaningful. I've decided—and I'm sure it's been proven somewhere—that it's better to sit and de-stress for five minutes than to spend those five minutes loading and unloading the dishwasher *again*. Granted, you don't want to live in a disaster zone, but your home doesn't have to be perfect.

✓ **Wind down your day.** Segue from work to family with a mini break. Maybe you start a routine where you put on some soothing music or get the kids to dance

Mood Foods

The right foods can help you to relax.

- **Oranges**: Vitamin C supports your immune system.
- **Pistachios**: A handful can lower your blood pressure.
- **Chocolate**: Hello???? Research has found that including just a little piece—not necessarily the dark kind—can make you happier.
- **Salmon**: Is rich in omega 3 fatty acids which are crucial for brain function.
- **Tea**: A cup of chamomile or peppermint soothes your anxieties as well as your stomach.
- **Turkey**: Thanks to the tryptophan, this is a feel-good hormone serotonin.
- **Red Wine**: Another no-brainer. A glass a day relaxes you—plus is good for your heart.

Cook with Style

Tayga Kitchen Aprons

Add some pizzaz and fun to cooking dinner with a reversible, fashionable apron by mom of two Pam Mischler (she even has kid sizes). Because Pam's a big believer in family meals—and stands behind *Dinner for Busy Moms*, she's offering readers 10% off their apron purchases. Go to Tayga Aprons.com and use coupon **busymoms** at checkout.

with you in the living room pre-dinner as a way to get everyone's sillies out and start the process of relaxing for the evening. Or maybe you stop for a latte or plug in your favorite Bruce Springsteen CD on your way home from work. I like to create a "no surprises" policy, whereby I call home on my way from my office so I can prep myself for what went on with everyone's day. This way I know what I'm walking in to (and what kind of mood my teenage girls will be in).

✔ **Leave your work mind behind.** Easier said than done. But you can be OFF for the two hours or so that it takes to prepare and eat dinner with your family and put the kids to bed.

✔ **Let go of jealousy and envy.** I'll admit it: I've always been jealous of my friend, Lynn, who has a clean house and dinner on the table every night. She doesn't have the same work schedule I do, but she does have a busy life. And of course, her kids eat 99.9 percent of their vegetables, and are happy to try new things. In the end, though, who does this hurt? Me. I have to learn to let go and concentrate on *my* life and *my* family.

✔ **Switch to healthy snacks.** Too much sugar and caffeine keep you ON when you need to be OFF. Start paying attention to the snacks you're putting in your body, and concentrate on better ones. You'll feel better when you eat better (and that means not skipping meals!).

Give your kids chores as a way to build responsiblity.

✔ **Delegate.** Remember to involve children with chores. This builds responsibility and helps them to feel needed. And, of course, your hubby can help too.

✔ **Scrub away tension.** Yeah, I know. . . A warm bubble bath is something all the women's magazines are always advising. (I know, I wrote for them for many years.) But if you *can* find 15 minutes in your day, or even five, it works. Refresh your body with a soothing bath when you can, or de-stress your hands by massaging them and putting on some sweet-smelling lotions. Even running your feet under warm water when you get home can help you shift moods and be a tad more peaceful.

Mom Tip

"Don't discount going out to eat—the family meal doesn't have to be at the kitchen table—if you're having good conversation and are feeling connected to each other— that's fine. Bear in mind: The drive-through doesn't count."

—Martha Marino, Director of Nutrition Affairs, Washington State Dairy Council, Lynnwood, WA, mom of two, ages 18 and 21

It's easy to forget our own needs, but you do need to be selfish, and that means getting enough rest.

Mom Tip

"Keep your grocery list on your smart phone, so you have it with you wherever you go. iPhones and Blackberries have grocery list apps that enable you to create a recurring list, organize lists by aisles, and put pictures of products you normally buy next to the item name."

—Jill Houk, Chicago, IL, mom of one, age 10, CenteredChef.com

✔ **Organize.** By clearing your space, you can clear your mind. Get organized by breaking large tasks into smaller, more manageable ones. Think of your energy drain as an invitation to recharge. Once you can see the calm after the storm, you'll have more energy to deal with stressful situations. Taiha Wagner suggests a meal-planning party (often a weeknight) with a bunch of girlfriends. Everyone brings the cheese, crackers, and one or two of their favorite recipes, photocopied. Not only do you have ten meals brainstormed out for you, but you have quality time with friends.

✔ **Be prepared.** We have the least energy and the highest demands between 4:30 and 6:30 p.m. That's when most of us face kids returning from school, commutes, pick-up from day care, food preparation, mail, errands, and evening schedules. This is also the peak time for food cravings, particularly chocolate. Plan for this low point. Stock the car or kitchen with water, fruit, and soothing music. If children are returning from school, stop everything for half an hour, and do nothing but help them transition to home.

✔ **Accept the facts.** The truth is, I know my kids think I've been put on this earth to serve them. I know I'm not getting thank-yous or gratitude or any of that until. . . well. . . until possibly they're parents themselves. And so, I'm learning to roll with it. I find that reading inspirational quotes every now and then (very Oprah, I know), puts things in perspective. Here's one of my faves:

> *"A mother is a person who, seeing there are only four pieces of pie for five people, promptly announces she never did care for pie."*
> –Tenneva Jordan

I love this quote because it says who we really are. As a mom, it's often not in our nature to put ourselves first. Depending on the age of your kids, it's not always practical either. Imagine saying "sorry" to your two-year-old because you need a time out. But if you don't figure out a way to make *your* life easier (maybe when Junior is napping?), you will become so overloaded and exhausted that, at some point, you'll lose it.

It's easy to forget, but you need to stay healthy, which means eating well and

Mom Tip

"My husband works a lot of nights, so he's not always around for dinner. Consistency is key for the kids. Even if Daddy's not home, mealtime together is what our family does."

—Shane Okoon Shaps, Louisville, KY, mom of two, ages 5 and 3

fyi

Sub veggies and beans for meat. Make lasagna with frozen chopped spinach, or replace half the ground beef with an equal amount of beans in chili. Just one way to add more varied nutrition to your kids' meals.

Mom Tip

"I try to pre-plan my meals. They have to be simple, like sautéed seasoned chicken breasts, with one of those bags of frozen veggies that you can pop in the microwave!"

—Lisa Spellman, Omaha, NE, mom of three, ages 5, 7, and 10

"Don't go crazy and force the food issue. Meal time should be a time of peace and togetherness for a family. Most of us have enough stress, why add more."

—Amanda Louden, Gold River, CA, mom of two, ages 5 and 7 (EatYourRoots.org)

getting a good night's sleep. Sometimes we get so busy that we skip meals or try to keep ourselves up later longer, but this is a bad idea. Your body needs the energy from food and sleep to keep it going, especially when things get hectic.

You Know More Than You Think You do

Consider this your "You're terrific whatever it is you're doing" section of the book. We busy moms aren't perfect—and we don't need to be. Some days we can manage the 6 p.m. scramble, stretch a recipe from one meal into two (or three), and manage to instill some kind of ritual into our evenings, and some nights we can't. And that's OK. That's what leftovers, frozen pizza and Chinese take-out is for. I love this quote from humorist Calvin Trillin: "The most remarkable thing about my mother is

Highly Recommended For Your Bookshelf

***Clueless in the Kitchen: A Cookbook for Teens and other Beginners* by Evelyn Raab**

Granted, the title says teens and, yes, many moms buy this for their kids as they go off to college, but for those with two left thumbs in the kitchen, it's a must. It's a great way, too, for you and your teen to learn to cook better together.

***How to Get Your Kid to Eat. . . But Not Too Much,* by Ellyn Satter.**

This is a book all parents should read, whether their children have eating problems or not. It applies to kids from birth through the teen years. The advice in this book can start your child off with a healthy relationship with food that will last a lifetime.

Turn to page 207 for more recommendations

that for thirty years she served the family nothing but leftovers. The original meal has never been found."

This kind of homage to Mom shows we women are able to make lemonade out of lemons no matter what, even if it means rummaging through our pantries to find dinner. We are the feeders of the soul as well as the ones who literally put food on the table. As expert Ellyn Satter says, you don't have to make grandmother's fried chicken and all the trimmings to make dinner a success. "We are talking about structure—and structure—and structure. A meal is a meal if you all sit down."

Thanks to the strategies outlined in this book, you're more organized, and more thoughtful when it comes to family meal planning. You've prioritized dinner in a way that makes a family a family with food, chores, conversation and connectiveness. High fives all around simply for trying. (I also encourage treating yourself to chocolate, wine or a spa treatment.) Other tricks to keep you on track follow.

Sanity Savers

* **Plan your weekly calendar.** Planning ahead doesn't have to be hard. This means figuring out your grocery list, when you can shop and what meals you'll plan for the week. If you're not into committing to a running meal plan or grocery list, simply get a bunch of index cards (say fourteen for two weeks), and write a meal and recipe on each one. Then shuffle the deck: Decide what to have each day, and post the card on your fridge.

Mom Tips

"Every morning on their way out the door, my boys ask, 'What's for dinner?' About a month ago, I had a brainstorm. On Sunday mornings, one of the kids is put in charge of making up a dinner menu for the week. All I have to do is prepare the shopping list (sometimes the kids do that too), and off I go to the market (like a happy idiot). The kids are happy because they get to eat what they like, and I'm happy because I don't have to come up with five meal ideas."
—Barbara Kimmel, Chester, NY, mom of two, ages 12 and 14

"On Sundays I plan all meals for the next ten days. I include about eight standards and add two new recipes. I always prepare the dinner in the morning before I leave for work. If we have mashed potatoes, I cut potatoes, leave them in water for the day, and cook them late in the afternoon. Anything I can pre-prepare, like soups or casseroles, I finish cooking in the morning and warm up at night."
—Anja DeGeorgia, Cleveland, OH, mom of three, ages 10, 12, and 14

Snacking Tips for Moms

I gained ten pounds when my kids were younger because I fed everyone in shifts—the kids first and my husband and me later. Which meant I ended up often eating two dinners—one with them and one with him, with plenty of snacks (and glasses of wine) along the way. Hello weight gain and, eventually, unhappiness with eating dinner twice. What I learned to do instead:

● **Snack on an apple.** Apples are filling and healthy. I'm also big on filling up with an apple and a teaspoon of peanut butter.

● **Stop eating standing up at the counter.** You never realize how much you're putting in your mouth.

● **Take a breath mint or piece of gum.** I'd pop this in my mouth when feeding my kids to avoid eating the French fries off their plates.

● **Wait 15 minutes.** Instead of giving in to my cravings, I'll make herbal tea, walk the dog, or do something else... away from the kitchen.

✶ **Have food accessible so you can cook it.**

✶ **The minute you get home from the supermarket, start chopping, cutting, slicing, and dicing right then**—put in storage containers so it's there for you and ready when you need it (or buy it sliced and diced). This sounds harder than it is—promise!

✶ **Think double-duty.** What works as a side dish? Main course? If you're cooking rice or potatoes, maybe those things can be substituted later in the week with another protein. Always think in the back of your mind: What can you cook once and eat twice?

✶ **Allow for flexibility.** Just because you plan doesn't mean you can't be spontaneous. Some moms don't like to meal plan for the simple reason that they may wake up Tuesday morning and no longer be in the mood for tacos. But if you planned and shopped smart at the grocery store, you can move things around, defrost items, pull from your pantry, and still have dinner in less than a half hour.

✶ **Use time-saving prepared ingredients,** such as prepared sauces, marinated meats, washed/pre-cut vegetables, bagged salads, and other lifesavers, such as frozen pre-cooked brown rice.

✶ **Use technology to your advantage.** Do shopping online. Set up alerts for what you need.

✶ **De-stress.** You're rushing, rushing , rushing, but have to stop dead when in the long grocery line at Costco. There's nothing you can do. So stay calm. Pop a mint

Expert Advice: Ellyn Satter's
Family-Friendly Meal-Planning Tactics

- Include all the food groups: Meat or other protein; a couple of starchy foods, fruit or vegetable or both; butter, salad dressing or gravy; and milk.

- Always offer plenty of bread or some other starch that family members like and can fill up on. That could be sliced bread, tortillas, pita, Indian flat bread, Asian pancakes or wraps, cornbread, biscuits, crackers, rice, potatoes, or pasta.

- Include high- and low-fat food in meals and snacks. This satisfies both big and small appetites.

- Make mealtimes pleasant. Make conversation. Don't scold or fight. Observe a division of responsibility in feeding.

- Regularly offer "forbidden food" in moderation (i.e., low-nutrient food such as sweets and chips).

- When you are ready, get more organized with cooking, planning, and shopping. However, don't get caught in virtue. Go back to step two or step three when you need to. Have the occasional cook's night off, and share popcorn and cocoa in front of the television. Remember, even the most ho-hum family meal is better than no meal at all.

COPYRIGHT © 2009 BY ELLYN SATTER. PUBLISHED AT ELLYNSATTER.COM. FOR MORE ABOUT FAMILY MEALS (AND FOR RESEARCH BACKING UP THIS ADVICE), SEE ELLYN SATTER'S SECRETS OF FEEDING A HEALTHY FAMILY: HOW TO EAT, HOW TO RAISE GOOD EATERS, HOW TO COOK, KELCY PRESS, 2008. ALSO SEE ELLYNSATTER.COM/SHOPPING, TO PURCHASE BOOKS AND TO REVIEW OTHER RESOURCES.

Cookies are allowed in moderation.

in your mouth. Be patient.

* **Make Time.** Don't over-schedule your kids. . . and don't over-schedule yourself to the point that dinner becomes an impossibility. When I think back on my childhood, I remember meals with my parents more than I remember a specific ballet recital or a piano lesson.

* **Accept the "best you can do."** It's a mantra I'm always saying to my kids. "Sorry, but this is the best I can do." Good enough is OK.

* **Phone a friend.** A good support system (and hearing someone else say they are overwhelmed and drowning in Domestic Goddess responsibilities is often all you need to deal. . . and remind yourself to crack a smile.)

* **Focus on what's good, rather than what's not.** So what if you burnt dinner and had to order pizza? So what if you're eating scrambled eggs while moving your stack of bills off the dining room because the kitchen table still has the breakfast dishes on top? Your kids are healthy. You have a roof over your heads. There's food in the freezer and cereal in the cabinet. You shouldn't judge yourself or let others judge you based on what you serve (or don't serve) for dinner.

* **Breathe.** Take time to breathe in and out. It sounds simple and New Age-y, I know, but one minute to simply inhale and focus on the moment can help.

7

Now We're Cooking!

Back in the old days dinner meant **mom, dad and kids sitting togeth- er promptly at 6 p.m.** for a meal of meat, potatoes, and a vegetable. Back then, there were no worries about what was laden with cholesterol or what was low-fat or fat-free. Fast forward to today, and dinner's quite a different experience. Kitchen counters have replaced tables; and children sit perched in front of their computer screens, or watching TV while mom and dad often shovel some-thing microwaveable into their mouths, (pos-sibly checking nutritional value and calorie count?) before they dash into the car to drive the kids to yet another enrichment activity or intramural sport.

Why We Need a Strategy

We've gone from an era of having noth-ing but time to being so completely time-pressed, that we no longer know how to slow down. And there's no bigger casualty than the

The era of the supermom is over: Let kids and partners pitch in and help.

family dinner. Which is why, when people ask me why busy women need a strategy approach to dinner when a plain ol' cookbook could do, I look them in the eye and tell them the truth: Moms are NOT born with a gene to "do it all effortlessly."

Sure, some of us may make it look easy, but behind every put-together mom is someone with a closet full of clothes from the '90s, more than a couple of junk drawers, and a list of "to dos" stuck on sticky-notes around the house. For those like me, that also means you're late with planning your daughter's next physical, you haven't been to the doctor yourself, and you can't remember the last time you had five minutes without hearing the word, "Moooooomm." We need help, not only to remind us how to carve time for ourselves, but to make us realize that we're not alone in the struggle to cater to our kids.

Becoming a mom and juggling whatever else you have in your life (work, aging parents, errands that need running, laundry, dry cleaning, etc.) means prioritizing. And sometimes, the things that mean the most—i.e., sitting down together as a family when you see each other at sporadic moments during the day—doesn't seem like something we need to plan. But we do. If we want to raise a generation of men and women who appreciate the value of food and family, then we need to make mealtimes as important an activity as your daughter's piano lessons, your son's baseball practices or your book clubs.

Food and family are intertwined with love

There's nothing quite as warmhearted as sitting around the table with those you share your life with. Heck, it's how my husband, Mark, started wooing me—by making ME dinner. With candlelight, I might add. Making food for someone, sitting down and being in the same space with your undivided attention proves to those around you that you believe in rituals and traditions.

Dinner is the glue that holds you together, no matter how hectic your lives are. Now, more than ever, when we communicate via email, IM's and Facebook pages, when we text rather than talk, we need to put face time at the top of our list. Dinner together is a simple way to connect as a family and a wonderful way to establish traditions your kids will appreciate long after they leave the house.

The truth is, before I streamlined meal planning and put dinner on the front burner, I had about ten cookbooks gathering dust on my shelf. I know how to cook—I did it a lot of it pre-children—but once I had kids and less time, it just didn't seem possible to find an extra half hour in the day to look at a recipe, let alone write down the ingredients, food shop, and throw the whole kiboodle together. I know the "why" behind the reasons I'd let dinnertime slip in our house, but I'd lost the "how."

If you came to my house five years ago you would have seen pizza for one daughter, rotisserie chicken for another, and a sub for my husband all sitting on the kitchen counter. Back then, my family ate dinner at separate times. A magazine story assignment finally launched me on this quest to bring back family dinners in my house. The more I talked to nutritional experts and women across the country, the more I heard how happy they were that I was writing about this subject.

"Dinner together is a lost art," one woman said. "I know teenagers who never eat with their families," said another, "which is why they like coming to our house. They tell me it's homey and that their mom never cooks." Another teen told me, "Dinner in my house means the food gets cooked and whoever is hungry eats when they want."

Granted, we all need to be realistic about what works for us. Dinner five nights a week may be an impossibility for some, but certainly you can try for one or two? Believe me: I'm not advocating perfection. We're nowhere near that in our house, but I'm trying. And I've gotten my kids into the act so they care and notice when there's a shift in plans.

Good food, good conversations, and laughter—that's what family dinners are supposed to be about. Hopefully, this book helped remind you of dinners growing up in your own family. . . or mealtimes that you saw—and pined for—on TV. (Hey, who wouldn't want to be at the Cosby family dinner table?) More than anything, I hope it gave you your "how" back.

Luckily, the era of the Super Mom is over

We're now in the decade of the "Real Mom:" The honest woman who knows she needs support from other family members and friends if she's also going to give her kids what they need, but also fulfill her own wants and desires. While we carry the bulk of the responsibility for the family meal, we are no longer—nor should we be—the sole providers. Children and spouses need to participate. Get kids engaged early on. Let them be a part of food shopping and planning. They can help pick out recipes, stock the pantry, and add to your running grocery list. We can also empower them about the foods we eat by growing our own, even if it's just herbs by the windowsill. And we certainly can give our husbands an eco-friendly shopping bag and a grocery list and send them on their way. One mom friend of mine often leaves her husband and teenage kids notes for how to heat up or add extras to a meal if they get home before she does.

In short, life can be hard, but dinnertime shouldn't be. You don't have to spend hours slaving over a hot stove, like women did in the '60s and '70s, nor do you have to rely on take-out every night. You just have to make a commitment to be together at a certain time on nights that work for you, and give yourself wiggle room to be flexible. All that chopping slicing, marinating, microwaving and defrosting may seem like mundane tasks, but believe me, they are the recipe for a swell of emotions and long-lasting memories.

Jeanne

P.S. I'd love to hear how you're redefining mealtimes in your house. Keep me posted at Jeanne@JeanneMuchnick.com.

Recipes and Resources

The moment of truth: Time to cook/
get everyone to the table. Honestly?
All that matters is that you're present
and that you have something for your kids to
eat. And yes, take-out counts. As author Ellyn
Satter writes, "The biggest error parents make
is that they underestimate how important they
are to their children." Establishing rituals, in-
stilling good eating habits, modeling healthy
behaviors, and spending time together is really what matters.

You Don't Need to Be a Chef

The best part? You don't have to be a great
cook. You simply have to learn to throw chick-
en in a marinade, beef in a crock pot, or roll
some meats in panko crumbs. To make it easy
for you, I've compiled a variety of foolproof
ideas—a recap of some of my favorite easy
recipes from some of my best go-to sources,
including my friend (and chef) Nisa Lee, a Pel-
ham, New York, mom of four and a full-time ca-
terer (NisaLee.com) who puts a sophisticated

Mom Tip

"I like to use the five-ingredient cookbooks, Rachel Ray recipes, and family recipes most often. Cookbooks written especially for kids also have some tasty, easy recipes. If you make chicken, fish, or pork as your main dish, you can change the side dishes often enough to keep things interesting. Once you have a collection of favorite recipes memorized, you can easily tweak them with new spices or accompaniments, and that keeps your meals from becoming boring."

—Diane Asyre, St. Louis, MO, mom of three, ages 10, 12 and 13

"All kids like spaghetti sauce. To add more nutrition, take the beans and veggies of your choice, mash/puree/liquefy it, and add a can or two of tomato paste or a jar of ready-made pasta sauce. This mixture is veggie-packed, good on pizza, chicken, cheese bread, or any pasta, and freezes very well. So you can make a big batch, then freeze it for future single-meal servings."

—Rebecca Fenlon, St Louis MO, mom of two, ages 13 months and 13.

spin on recipes that can also double as great party fare, and Janice Newell Bissex and Liz Weiss, registered dietitians and the two gurus behind the website The Meal Makeover Moms (MealMakoverMoms.com). I seriously love everything these women do as their recipes are straightforward, quick, and make me look like a star.

Thanks to my publishing background, I have friends in the industry: Jennifer Perillo, a food editor, consultant and blogger (go to In JenniesKitchen.com) is one of them, and her website is forever challenging me to come up with fresh ideas, often using my local farmer's market. I also rely on Cornelia Zell, Pampered Chef extraordinaire, who used to work in the magazine world but ventured out on her own and established herself as the "go-to" cook in my Westchester County, New York, neighborhood. And though Atlanta moms Iris Feinberg and Lynn Epstein, created a cookbook with the motto, *No More Frozen Pizza*, and I believe wholeheartedly in frozen pizza, I like the thought process behind their recipes: No fuss ideas meant to simplify the cooking process. Plus, the book is really recipe cards served in a pizza box so how can you not like that?

Because I love Trader Joe's, I'm forever turning to *Cooking with Trader Joe's*, written by two California moms. When I pick up their recipes I know they'll be do-able as I only have to go to one store. And, because I love my freezer, I've embraced the website and ideas of Tricia Callahan, a mom of two from Dayton, Ohio, who runs the website OnceA MonthMom.com and believes in batch cooking. I also follow foodie Vanessa Druckman, aka Chef Druck, a Columbus, Ohio, mom of three (ChefDruck.com), who I admire for having three young children with growing gourmet tastes.

Since some moms (i.e., my sister) are adventurous, I've included something from a restaurant owner in White Plains, New York, who runs a sandwich shop and does cooking classes for moms on the side. Bill Hall and Kristin Mulrane, owners of Melt Sandwich shop (and yes, the sandwiches literally melt in your mouth), promised me pasta was an affordable, easy to make dinner solution, and though I thought I could NEVER do something this complicated, their recipe turned into a small miracle of accomplishment for me, so I've included it for you.

And since, we moms often have "whine" with dinner (and therefore need our own wine), a glass of cheers and thanks to Stuart Levine, wine columnist and owner of Vino 100 wine boutique in White Plains NY, who gave me suggestions on what wines go best with the meals provided. Look for the wine icons for suggested pairings a the end of each recipe.

Frankly, when I started this journey, I didn't think I could do any of this. But once I got into the habit of fitting dinner into our day, it became something that slowly became part of our routine. And yes, I have to admit I'm impressed with myself, though my clean-up process still needs work. There's a security and sense of calm in knowing you have a healthy meal in the freezer, in the pantry, or in the crock pot, as well as a sense of happiness and acomplishment when you see your family's faces gathered around the table. And, of course, I love that when my kids ask "What's for dinner?" I finally have an answer.

Send in your recipes!

We want to hear from you. Especially because we think the next generation of this book should be *Dinner Recipes for Busy Moms*. Submit your quickest, easiest, most delicious family-pleasers at Jeanne@JeanneMuchnick.com.

Measurements

tablespoon (tbsp.)	3 teaspoons (tsp.)
1/16 cup	1 tablespoon
1/8 cup	2 tablespoons
1/6 cup	2 tablespoons + 2 teaspoons
1/4 cup	4 tablespoons
1/3 cup	5 tablespoons + 1 teaspoon
3/8 cup	6 tablespoons
1/2 cup	8 tablespoons
2/3 cup	10 tablespoons + 2 teaspoons
3/4 cup	12 tablespoons
1 cup	48 teaspoons
1 cup	16 tablespoons
8 fluid ounces (fl oz.)	1 cup
1 pint (pt.)	2 cups
1 quart (qt.)	2 pints
4 cups	1 quart
1 gallon (gal.)	4 quarts
16 ounces (oz.)	1 pound (lb)
1 milliliter (ml.)	1 cubic centimeter (cc)
1 inch (in.)	2.54 centimeters (cm

Cell Phone Know-How

Cell phones are the new hot kitchen tool. Use them to text yourself a grocery list, convert recipe measurements on the calculator, snap a photo of a meal to send to a friend, or set the timer so you know when to take dinner out of the oven.

Setting the Table

* Set your dinner plate in the center

* The dinner fork goes directly to the left of the dinner plate.

* The salad fork goes to the left of the dinner fork

* Place napkins (folded into a rectangle or triangle), to the left of both forks.

* The knife, blade facing inwards, is to the right of the dinner plate.

* The spoon should be placed to the right of the dinner knife.

* The wine or water glass goes at the one o'clock
pos-ition, with respect to the dinner plate.

Give your kids chores by teaching them how to set the table.

My Standby Go-To Recipe

Jeanne's Mustard Chicken

- ❑ ½ cup (or more) Dijon mustard
- ❑ 6 boneless skinless chicken breasts
- ❑ 1½ cups breadcrumbs
- ❑ salt and pepper

This is my foolproof "something easy" that never fails me. And because I keep chicken breasts in the freezer and always have mustard and bread crumbs on hand, it's the perfect standby meal.

Wash and pat dry the chicken breasts. Put them in a bowl with mustard, salt and pepper and let sit in fridge for ½ hour. (Ideally you can do this step in the morning and let breasts marinate most of the day.) I also add a little water to the marinade so it isn't too thick.

Roll chicken in breadcrumbs, and bake 20-25 minutes at 375° oven until slightly crispy.

You can add more salt and pepper to taste. Serves 4-6.

Red: Pinot Noirs, try ones from Oregon or France to mix with the tang of the mustard. White: Alsatian Pinot Gris.

A Great Crock Pot Meal

Slow Cooked Barbeque Beef

Ingredients

- ❏ 2 lbs. lean stew meat
- ❏ 1 medium onion, diced
- ❏ 1 cup pitted prunes
- ❏ 1 cup all-natural barbecue sauce
- ❏ 8 to 10 whole wheat hamburger buns, toasted

I've sung the praises of the crock pot and here's just one reason why: You can throw everything in the pot in the morning, and come home later, and dinner's ready.

Add the meat, onion, prunes, and barbecue sauce to the slow cooker, and stir to combine. Cover and cook on low for 6 to 8 hours. When the meat is done, use two forks to pull the meat and prunes into shredded pieces. Divide the mixture evenly between the hamburger buns, and serve. *Serves 8 to 10.*

Tip: My kids actually like it better just served over medium-size egg noodles (no hamburger bun necessary). I also like it sans bun but with a baked potato on the side (and bread to sop up the sauce). My husband's suggestion: Add more veggies, and serve with rice. All ways it's delicious and super-easy.

Red: California Zinfandels. White: a tropical-fruit flavored Chardonnay from California's Santa Barbara County.

15-Minute Meal

Spicy Tropical Shrimp Boats

Ingredients

- ❑ 1 cup frozen, medium, cooked, tail-off shrimp, thawed
- ❑ ½ cup fire-roasted papaya mango salsa (or another mango salsa if you don't have a Trader Joe's by you)
- ❑ Salt and pepper
- ❑ 1 head fresh Belgian endive, leaves separated
- ❑ 2 tablespoons refrigerated cilantro dressing
- ❑ Cilantro for garnish

You can literally walk in the door from work and have this ready in less than half an hour. Plus, you don't need utensils to eat it.

Dice shrimp into cubes. Mix shrimp and salsa. Season with salt and pepper to taste. Spoon shrimp mixture onto endive leaves. Arrange shrimp boats on serving platter, and drizzle with dressing. Garnish with cilantro.

Variation: For a more traditional (and less spicy) shrimp salad, use ¼ cup cilantro dressing or other creamy dressing instead of the fruit salsa. Garnish with cilantro. *Serves 4 (2 boats each)*

FYI: If you can't find mango salsa or cilantro dressing. . . no worries. Try something else a tad fruity like peach salsa, and add scallions and cucumber. My friend's husband even liked it with jalapenos. He drizzled oil and vinegar on top, and she drizzled a creamy dressing.

White: Riesling or Gewurtztraminer. Red: Beaujolais Village or a California Pinot Noir, slightly chilled.

REPRINTED WITH PERMISSION FROM CA-BASED MOMS DEANA GUNN AND WONA MINIATI, AUTHOR OF COOKING WITH TRADER

For Big-Batch Easy-to-Freeze Cooking

Chicken Macaroni Bake

- ❏ ¼ cup onions, chopped
- ❏ 2 tablespoons butter or margarine
- ❏ ¼ cup milk
- ❏ 10 ½ oz. cream of chicken soup
- ❏ 1½ cups chicken or turkey, cooked and cubed
- ❏ 4 oz. cheddar cheese, shredded
- ❏ 8 oz. pasta, any variety, cooked
- ❏ 1/8 cup buttered bread crumbs

This dish is filling and ideal for doubling and freezing. Plus, chicken and pasta are two of my family's favorites.

Prepare pasta according to package directions. Brown onion in butter. Stir in soup, chicken, milk, and ¾ cups cheese; heat until cheese melts. Blend sauce with cooked noodles; pour into buttered baking dish. Mix the remaining cheese and bread crumbs and place on top. Bake at 350° for 30 minutes or until hot. *Serves 4-6*

Freezing Instructions
Prepare up to the point of baking—DO NOT BAKE. Place foil on baking dish and write the following instructions: Remove foil. Bake at 350° for 30 minutes (if thawed) or 1 hour (if frozen) or until hot.

Tip: Add frozen mixed veggies for a one-meal deal

 White: Soave from Veneto, Italy or a Tuscan Vernaccia di San Gim. Red: Italian chianti classico or Spanish Tempranillo.

For Something Hearty and Easy

Beef (or Turkey) Barley Stew

Ingredients

- ❏ 1 lb. lean ground beef (can substitute ground turkey)
- ❏ 2/3 cup of barley, rinsed
- ❏ 2 cans Veg-All®
- ❏ 3 cups V-8® or tomato juice
- ❏ 1 medium potato, peeled and cut into ½" cubes
- ❏ 3 cups water
- ❏ 1 teaspoon Italian seasonings
- ❏ ½ teaspoon pepper
- ❏ Add other seasonings to taste, such as salt, garlic, parsley

Anything that means throwing a bunch of stuff together into a pot is a winner in my book.

Brown ground beef in small stock pot. Drain grease. Add other ingredients and simmer until barley is cooked, about 45 minutes. *Serves 4-6*

FYI: Veg-all® can be found in your grocery store's canned veggie section; it's basically just a combination of a bunch of vegetables; you can also find them frozen. This was easy to put together but does take time to simmer, making it ideal for something to cook on Sunday—with enough for leftovers later in the week.

 Red: Earthy, country wines like Cotes du Rhone or Bordeaux. White: Chardonnay from Burgundy.

Favorite Standby

Honey Roast Chicken

- ❑ 4 tablespoons butter
- ❑ 1½ tablespoons honey
- ❑ 1 egg yolk
- ❑ 3 lbs. chicken pieces
- ❑ ½ teaspoon garlic powder
- ❑ 2 teaspoons salt
- ❑ ¼ teaspoon pepper

Easy to double and freeze

We eat a lot of chicken in our house. This is a simple recipe that is basically fool-proof.

Preheat oven to 325°. In a small microwave-safe bowl, melt the butter in the microwave for one minute or until melted. Let cool for two minutes, then add the honey and egg yolk, and mix well. Spray a large pan with cooking spray. Put the chicken in the pan, skin side down, and sprinkle with garlic powder, salt, and pepper. Spoon the honey mixture over the chicken. Bake for 45 minutes. Take the pan out of the oven and turn the chicken pieces over. Bake for another 15 minutes. *Serves 4-6*

Tip: In my oven, the chicken worked best when put on a middle rack. . . too close to the top and that butter mixture will burn the skin right up. I also felt the chicken could use a dash more flavor, so I put the butter-honey sauce underneath the skin.

 White: A dry Riesling from Alsace, France or a lighter red blend from Portugal or a fruity Malbec.

An Easy Summer Meal Ideal for Dinner or Lunch

Perfect Picnic Salad

Ingredients

- ❏ 3 cups of rice or couscous
- ❏ 3 ripe tomatoes, coarsely chopped, or 1½ cups of cherry tomatoes, sliced in half
- ❏ 1 can of corn
- ❏ 1 can of tuna, preferably in olive oil
- ❏ 3 hard-boiled eggs, coarsely chopped
- ❏ 2 stalks of celery, chopped finely
- ❏ Juice of ½ lemon
- ❏ ¼ cup of fresh parsley, chopped finely.

I love food that you can mix quickly and use for lunch the next day.

Except for the lemon and parsley, mix all the ingredients in one big bowl. Squeeze the lemon on top, and sprinkle the parsley. Serve chilled. *Serves 4*

Optional additional items: avocado, white beans, olives.

Tip: For a little extra healthiness, you can serve this in iceberg lettuce bowls.

 White: A Pinot Grigio or Portuguese Vinho Verde. Red: a slightly chilled Pinot Noir or Beaujolais Village.

DINNER FOR BUSY MOMS   193

Recycling aka "Loving Leftovers"

Vegetable Fried Rice

- ❑ 1 Tablespoon oil, plus more as needed for cooking
- ❑ 1 large egg, lightly beaten
- ❑ 1 small onion, chopped
- ❑ 1 carrot, diced ¼-inch
- ❑ ½ cup sliced baby bell mushrooms
- ❑ ¼ cup frozen peas
- ❑ 4 cups leftover white rice
- ❑ 4 teaspoons soy sauce
- ❑ 1 teaspoon oyster sauce
- ❑ 1 teaspoon sesame oil
- ❑ Salt & freshly ground pepper, to taste
- ❑ ¼ cup sliced scallions

This is an easy (and tasty) way to use leftover cooked rice. Just add a few Asian ingredients, last night's chicken or meat, and voila: A nutritious meal with hidden veggies for the kids. Ideal, too, because no wok is necessary; just use a non-stick skillet.

In a small bowl, whisk the soy sauce, oyster sauce, and sesame oil together; set aside. *Serves 4-6*

Heat 1 oil in a wok or deep skillet over medium-high heat. Add onions, carrots, and mushrooms, and sauté until golden, about 5 minutes. Add peas to wok, and stir-fry for 1 minute. Push vegetables to outer sides of wok or skillet, and heat another teaspoon of oil over medium-heat. Add egg and use a chopstick or fork to scramble.

Continued on next page

Vegetable Fried Rice

Continued from previous page

Add rice and remaining oil, plus more if rice is still too sticky, and stir fry vigorously to mix well and break up any large clumps of rice. Pour reserved soy sauce mixture over rice, and stir well to coat. Season with salt and pepper. Add scallions, toss well, and serve while hot.

Tip: There are a lot of ways you can spice up/add to this recipe, which is why I like it. Ideally, I'd add chicken and double the sauce so you can add more, according to taste preference. You could also add tofu or shrimp to get more protein. To save time, make rice ahead of time, or at the same time if you don't have enough left over from previous meals. Kids can even take leftovers for school lunch.

White: An Austrian Gruner Veltliner.
Red: A French Cotes du Rhone.

Picky Eater Pleaser

Mini Thai Tacos

- ❑ 1 package of wonton skins (found in ethnic aisle at grocery store, Asian grocery, or gourmet store).
- ❑ Mini cupcake baking pan (regular size cupcake pans can also be used)
- ❑ 1 pound of lean ground beef (or ground chicken, turkey, or chopped up vegetables)
- ❑ 1 packet of chili or taco seasoning
- ❑ 1 tablespoon of chopped red pepper
- ❑ 1 tablespoon of chopped scallions
- ❑ ¼ teaspoon Fire and Spice sauce (you can use a poultry or meat sauce or buy online at NisaLee.com)

This quick and fun dinner recipe is one of those young kids will enjoy helping you with. It can also be offered as hors d'oeuvres or as a vegetarian option. Plus, you can store the crispy wonton shells in an airtight container for up to one month, making it one of those staple items you always on hand.

Making the shells:

Preheat oven to 375°. On a dry flat surface, place a ⅓-cup measuring cup or small glass rim side-down onto a wonton skin. Use a sharp knife to cut along the rim to make a circle. Place the wonton skin circles in the mini cupcake baking pan, and bake for 5-7 minutes until light brown. When finished, the wonton skin will form the shape of a small cup, and the texture will feel light

Continued on next page

Mini Thai Tacos

Continued from previous page

and crispy. Set aside and let cool. You can make the shells ahead of time and place them in an air tight container.

For the filling:

Sauté the ground beef in a pan over medium heat until cooked about 7-9 minutes. Follow directions from the chili or taco seasoning packet.

Assembly:

Place about a tablespoon of the filling in wonton shell. Garnish with the scallion and red pepper for color. Top each taco with ¼ teaspoon of the Fire and Spice sauce. *Serves 8-10*

Tip: Add legumes (black, pinto, or kidney). Rinse the beans, add ¼ cup of chicken or vegetable stock, bring to a boil for about two to three minutes. Mash or puree it with a mixer. Scoop pureed beans in shells before topping it with the meat or vegetables, or simply serve as a side option. You can find Thai sauces available for shipping ot NisaLee.com. It's an easy way to turn something standard into something exotic.

White: Either a Riesling, a Vouvray (a semi-dry Chenin Blanc from the Loire Valley). Red: a slightly chilled fruity red blend from California, or sangria.

To Challenge Yourself

Homemade Whole Wheat Pasta

- ❏ 2 cups 100% whole wheat flour such as Gold Medal® 100% Whole Wheat flour.
- ❏ 4 egg whites
- ❏ 2 tablespoons water
- ❏ 2 pinches of salt

This recipe is a bit more challenging but because it's so versatile—who doesn't love pasta—it's a crowd pleaser and worth it for those Sunday afternoons when you're in the mood to cook. It takes practice, but once you accomplish this, you'll feel great.

Place all ingredients in a food processor and blend with the dough blade for about 45 seconds. The dough will not come together.

Remove ingredients from the processor. Use your hands to form the dough into a ball. Let rest about 5 minutes.

Divide the dough into 4 equal

Continued on next page

Whole Wheat Pasta

Continued from previous page

balls. Using a rolling pin, roll out each ball into approximately a 9 x 12 rectangle. (While rolling out the dough you will need to dust the dough with a little flour.)

Dust each pasta sheet with a little flour. Roll each sheet into a tube. Cut each tube into strands of pasta about the width of your pinkie finger. Gently toss to loosen. The pasta should look like fettuccine.

In a large pot of boiling water cook the pasta until *al dente* (still slightly firm) or to taste. (For the fresh whole wheat pasta recipe, that is about 45 seconds).

Drain into a colander and toss with accompanying topping, such as the roasted vegetable topping recipe or your favorite pasta sauce.

Serve and enjoy!

 See wine pairings for Roasted Vegetable topping, next page.

To Challenge Yourself

Roasted Vegetable Topping

- ❑ 1 turnip, peeled and diced
- ❑ 1 rutabaga, peeled and diced
- ❑ 1 onion, peeled and diced
- ❑ 2 tablespoons olive oil to drizzle
- ❑ salt and fresh ground pepper to taste
- ❑ 2 tablespoons butter
- ❑ 4 tablespoons olive oil
- ❑ 4 garlic cloves, minced
- ❑ 10 fresh sage leaves, sliced
- ❑ 1 small bag baby spinach
- ❑ 4 tablespoons grated parmesan

This recipe creates a hearty, delicious, and nutritious topping for the pasta, but it's also delicious served as a side dish.

Pre-heat oven to 350°

Place the diced turnip, rutabaga, and onion in a bowl. Toss with olive oil, and season with salt and pepper. Place on cookie sheet, and roast until tender. (about 25 minutes)

In a large sauté pan melt the butter and olive oil. Add the garlic, and cook on low heat until rendered (melted down) (about 5 minutes). Add the fresh sage, and set to the side.

Continued on next page

Roasted Vegetable Topping

Continued from previous page

Return heat to the sauté pan with the butter, garlic, sage, and olive oil. Add the roasted root vegetables. Add the cooked pasta. Add the spinach and toss to coat. Add the grated parmesan. Taste and adjust the seasoning with salt and pepper.

Red: A Nero D'Avola.
White: A Cattarato blend, both from Sicily.

Microwave-Ready

Basic Microwaved Mashed Potatoes

- ❑ 1 1/4 lbs. Russet potatoes*
- ❑ 1/2 cup each: nonfat plain yogurt and fat-free milk
- ❑ 1 1/2 tablespoons healthy butter spread
- ❑ 1/4 teaspoon sea salt (or 1/2 teaspoon garlic or seasoned salt)
- ❑ Freshly ground pepper to taste

*Yukon Gold, yellow or white potatoes can be substituted

I love potatoes: Easy to make...and even better. . . easy for your kids to make. I also love my microwave. Which is why this wonderful comfort food is a staple at our house. Plus, it only takes about 20 minutes.

Place whole potatoes (do not poke) into microwave-safe dish. Cover dish. (If covering dish with plastic wrap, poke small hole in plastic.) Microwave on HIGH for 10 to 12 minutes depending on strength of microwave. Use oven mitts to remove dish from microwave; carefully remove cover and mash well. Stir in yogurt, milk, butter spread and seasonings. Cook for a minute or more to heat if necessary. *Serves 4*

White: a nice buttery Chardonnay from the Russian River valley in Sonoma. Red: A Merlot or Cabernet Franc from Long Island.

Resources

I'm all about asking friends and friends of friends their go-to places for recipes, savings, ideas... after all, I think we busy moms are the best sourcese. (Reminder: I'd love to get your recipes so we can put in a *Busy Moms* Cookbook that's written by you! Write to me at jeanne@JeanneMuchnick.com.)

In the meantime, here are some other go-to places, recommended by moms and other foodie experts.

⏺ Mom sites I swear by:

* **ChefDruck.blogspot.com** A French Foodie recently transplanted from NJ to the Midwest with her husband and three kids who offers insight into recipes and parenting and overall offers inspiration in the kitchen

* **DinnerPlanner.com** If you want to pay for a subscription (about $15 for three months), you'll get professional help in creating a weekly dinner menu, complete with a shopping list. Members choose from a list of recipes, and DinnerPlanner. com prepares a list of ingredients

* **DIY-Food.com** Mom blogher Lindsay Maines aims to bridge the gap between the realities of time constraints and the need to be fed "real food." I love her old-fashioned comfort ideals with the hope of feeding our kids (and ourselves) food without harmful chemicals and stuff we can't pronounce

* **EatYourRoots.org** Nutrition education and advocacy from a mom of two whose mission is to feed her children "real" foods. You go girl!

* **FamilyFoodies.com** A weekly podcast and fun resource site for families who want to enjoy and improve meal time

* **FixFreezeFeast.com** Everything you need to know about freezer meals. And yes, its two moms leading the charge

* **theFoodNanny.com** Honest, realistic meal plans, ideas, and recipes from food guru Liz Edmunds

* **MaxLifeTherapies.com** Nutritionist, and mom of Max, Julie Hammerstein is like your personal health coach. She has some amazing informational and fun youtube videos at MaxMinutes.com

* **MealMakeoverMoms.com** One of my favorite sites filled with easy and do-able recipes from two honest and realistic women

* **MealPlanningMommies.com** Three moms who met over cheese dip and grapes one summer back in their college days now offer cooking and meal planning skills with frugal tips, recipes, blogs, and more

* **MenuFortheWeek.com** An on-time, on-budget, online dinner planner

* **MomsDinnerHelper.com** A forum for moms to talk turkey. . . and other dinner strategies

* **MomsMealConnection** A mom of five who's "been there/done that" offers free tips for planning weekly menus, grocery shopping and recipes

* **MyCoachLaurie.com.** Helpful nutritional tips from stepmom of one, Laurie Beebe

* **aNutritionMission.com** A mom of sons with special dietary needs who—bonus!–is a nutritionist, offers online help, support, as well as tons of useful information on what's healthy, feeding picky eaters, and dealing with special needs

* **OnceaMonthMom.com** A blog that focuses on cooking a majority of the month's meals in one day, with tips, recipes, and even menu plans for baby food

* **ParentingPower.ca** Tools and coaching for all your parenting needs

* **RosaBerry.com** A culinary school educated mom blogs about food and recipes

* **SarahCucinaBella.com** A mom of two blogs about food, family and creating memories in the kitchen. I love that she shows you what doesn't work, along with what does

* **SmallBitesOnline.com** Teaches parents how to make healthy, safe and sustainable food choices in a way that saves them time

* **theSpicedLife.blogspot.com** Musings from the kitchen of mom of two Laura Tabacca with great tips on books she's reading and kitchen stuff she loves

* **SuperKidsNutrition.com** Helpful tips suggestions on eating healthy outlined in a fun, creative way

* **ThisWeekForDinner.com** A California blogger who turned her weekly meal plans into a helpful way for other moms to plan dinner and share weekly meals

* **theVeggieQueen.com** Jill Nussinow, mom and registered dietician offers tons of vegetable enthusiasm and advice on cooking

$ Money-Saving:

* **CouponMom.com** A mom who's trying to help world hunger while also saving you big bucks

* **Coupons.com** More coupons

* **DealCatcher.com** A great way to sit on your couch, click and save

* **DealSeekingMom.com** "Real Deals for Real Moms" and real good

* **FrugalUpstate.com** Great tips on saving money, not only at the grocery store but in all walks of life

* **theGroceryGame.com** A frugal hobby gone global

* **GroceryGuide.com** Ways to find local savings at a supermarket near you

* **MamboSprouts.com** A site for organic deals

* **MyGroceryDeals.com** Store circulars from all 50 states, so you can search for sales at a store near you

* **OrganicGroceryDeals.com** A new community focused on organic foods and savings

* **Priceable.com** A grocery price comparison website

* **SmartChoice.com** And more coupons

* **SuddenlyFrugal.wordpress.com** Author (and mom of two) Leah Ingram writes about how to save money in all walks of life, a real value not only for cooking but life in general

Bookmark these: Recipe specific websites:

* **101Cookbooks.com** recipe blog

* **5DollarDinners.com** A mom of three who's big into couponing, grocery shopping and blogging

* **AllRecipes.com** Just what is says: all kinds of everyday recipes, plus the fancy stuff for those who like challenges

* **Boboli.com** More than pizza: Info on healthy eating, lifestyle choices and recipes

* **CampbellsKitchen.com** Easy recipes that you can make with Campbells products

* **Crock-Cook.com** Easy crock pot ideas

* **Crockpot365.blogspot.com** Writer Stephanie O'Dea blogs about her year of cooking with the crockpot—and has a book to boot

* **Epicurious.com** A go-to for anything and everything food and a big mom favorite

* **FoodNetwork.com** A staple

* **HealthyPantry.com** Healthy, affordable family meal kits: All you need to do is add the meat

* **Hersheys.com** More than chocolate: Fun ideas for cooking with kids

* **MellyBeeWellness.com** Natural Foods Chef Melinda Beaulieu can help you jumpstart your family on a healthy eating path

* **MyRecipes.com** An easy way to find something healthy and easy

* **PotatoGoodness.com** All you need to know about America's favorite vegetable

* **RealSimple.com** Offers new meal plans each month

* **RealWorkingMom.com/recipes.htm** If the kid on the front page with the chocolate mustache doesn't warm the cockles of your heart, nothing will

* **RecipeZaar.com** Numerous recipes, but rated so you can see what other people are saying (as in this dish needs more salt, less spices)

* **RiceaRoni.com** Offers your very own "Dinner Wizard" where you can transform the staples in your pantry into a delicious meal

* **Stouffers.com, LetsFixDinner.com,** The food company has a special section on dinner for families, with easy, affordable recipes

* **SuperCook.com** Search for recipes by what ingredients you have on hand

* **TasteBook.com** Print your own cookbook

* **TasteOfHome.com** A popular site with a range of innovative and easy ideas

Other Need to Know Websites

* **CasaFamilyDay.org** A national initiative to remind parents that waht kids really want at the dinner table is you

* **CoopDirectory.org** or **LocalHarvest.org/food-coops** and **nal.usda.gov/afsic/pubs/csa/csa.shtml** Information on CSA's

* **GoodGuide.com** Provides ratings of healthy products

* **Family-to-Family.org** A great way to enlist your family in community service.

* **EatSmart.org** Information and recipes from the Washington State Dairy Council

* **EllynSatter.com** Ideas on feeding your family and trusting your instincts

* **FDA.gov** Information and more from the Food and Drug Administration

* **FoodNews.org** A guide to pesticides in produce

* **FoodSafety.gov** Food safety details

* **GreenPeople.org** Plug in your zipcode and find a CSA (Community Supported Agriculture) co-op near you

* **JacksHarvest.com** Frozen organic baby food information and products

* **MeatAMI.com** News from the American Meat Institute

* **MyPyramid.gov** For menu planning, cooking tips, etc.

* **Organic.org** Details on organic food

* **OrganicItsWorthIt.com** The official website of the Organic Trade Association

* **StillTasty.com** Invaluable info on food storage—plus fun food tips

On the shelf: Book recommendations

* **29 Minutes to Dinner** by The Pampered Chef. I continue to be impressed with the ease of their recipes

* **The American Vegetarian Cookbook from the Fit for Life Kitchen** by Marilyn Diamond. More than just recipes, a healthy guide to eating right

* **Artisan Bread in 5 Minutes a Day** *and* **Healthy Bread in 5 Minutes a Day** by Jeff Herzberg & Zoe Francois. If you can find time, the warm smell of bread in the house is often all you need to feel good about dinner. Add soup and salad and you're set

* **The Barefoot Contessa** Series by Ina Garten. Pick one, any one, they're all great, though I love *Family Style* the best

* **Barrone's Food Lover's Companion** by Sharon Tyler Herbst. Not a cookbook, but a great reference to have

* **Betty Crocker's Picture Cookbook** A classic staple for every kitchen *and* **Betty Crocker's Dinner for Two Cookbook** Good for single moms

* **Bobby Flay's Grill It!** by Bobby Flay. Because who doesn't love grilling? And ditto for **Italian Grill** by Mario Batali with Judith Sutton

* **Chicken Soup for the Soul: Recipes for Busy Moms** by Jack Canfield. Specifically targeted for the on-the-go mom with easy recipes that even the non-cook like me can do

* **Desperation Dinners** by Beverly Mills and Alicia Ross. Let's just say I wish I had written this book. It's my bible

* **The Everything Slow Cooker Cookbook** by Margaret Kaeter. Slow cooker meals are a busy mom's dream

* **Food to Live By** by Myra Goodman. Just great, healthy food

* **A Good Day For Soup** by Jeannette Ferrary and Louise Fiszer (Author). More than 200 ideas for soup

* **How to Cook Everything** and **Kitchen Express** by Mark Bittman. If I weren't married, I'd be in love. His stuff is awesome

* **Make It Fast, Cook It Slow: The Big Book of Everyday Slow Cooking** by Stephanie O'Dea. Think the premise behind the book Julie and Julia where a food blogger aims to make every Julia Child recipe and gets a movie and a bestseller out of the deal. Now fast forward to December 2007 when Stephanie O'Dea made a New Year's resolution: she'd use her slow cooker every single day for an entire year, and blog about it. The result: more than 300 fabulous, easy-to-make, family-pleasing recipes. A MUST!

* **The Martha Stewart Cookbook** A bit ambitious for me, but many foodie moms swear by it

* **The New Moosewood Cookbook** by Mollie Katzen. Most dishes in here can be done in less than an hour. Plus the author's conversational tone makes this a keepsake

* **No More Frozen Pizza by Iris Feinberg and Lynn Epstein:** Talk about fun and easy! I love that these two moms know kids. . . Plus how can you not love a recipe book that's packaged in a pizza box.

* **Not Your Mother's Slow Cooker Cookbook** by Beth Hensperger and Julie Kaufmann. Comfort food done easy

* **Preserved** by Nick Sandler and Johnny Acton. Info on bringing out the best in preserved foods

* **Secrets of Feeding a Healthy Family** by Ellyn Satter. I love her philosophies that celebrate eating

* **The Sneaky Chef** by Missy Chase Lapine FAB ways to sneak veggies and fruits into your kids (and hubby's) meals

* **Sneaky Veggies** by Chris Fisk. Another easy way to add veggies to your family's diet

* **Stop Dieting and Lose Weight** by Anne Egan and Regina Ragone, R.D. I worked with Anne a million years ago at *Woman's World Magazine* and tasted her recipes first-hand. I love ALL her books (and food!). Google her and you'll find lots more

* **Taste of Home: The New Appetizer** (Reader's Digest). When you're in the mood for comfort food and that taste of home

Index

Website Index